CRABTREE & EVELYN COOKBOOK

CRABTREE & EVELYN COOK BOOK

A BOOK OF LIGHT MEALS
AND SMALL FEASTS

❧

PHOTOGRAPHS BY
CHRISTOPHER BAKER

❧

STEWART, TABORI & CHANG
NEW YORK

Text copyright © Crabtree & Evelyn, Ltd. 1989
Photographs copyright © 1989 Christopher Baker
Design and illustrations copyright © 1989 Peter Windett

Published in 1989 by
Stewart, Tabori & Chang, Inc.
740 Broadway, New York, New York 10003

Library of Congress Cataloging-in-Publication Data

Crabtree & Evelyn cook book : a book of light meals and
small feasts / photographs by Christopher Baker.
    p.   cm.
    Includes index.
    ISBN 0-941434-99-0
    1. Cookery. 2. Crabtree & Evelyn (Firm) I. Baker,
Christopher. II. Crabtree & Evelyn (Firm) III. Title: Crabtree
and Evelyn cook book.
TX714.C72 1989
641.5′68—dc19   89-30646
                                                       CIP

Distributed in the U.S. by Workman Publishing,
708 Broadway, New York, New York 10003

Distributed in Canada by Canadian Manda Group, P.O. Box
920 Station U, Toronto, Ontario M8Z 5P9

Distributed in all other territories by Little, Brown and
Company, International Division, 34 Beacon Street, Boston,
Massachusetts 02108

Edited by Elizabeth Kent
Designed by Peter Windett

Printed in Japan
10 9 8 7 6 5 4 3 2 1

The illustrations reproduced on the following pages were
selected from copyrighted Crabtree & Evelyn packaging from
the years 1973–1988. Reproduction is by permission of the
copyright owner, Crabtree & Evelyn, Ltd. We are grateful for
the help and enthusiasm we have had from all the artists and
we would especially like to thank:

John Astrop
Ian Beck
Glynn Boyd-Harte
Braldt Bralds
Peter Brookes
Malcolm Chandler
Peter Church
Alan Cracknell
Fiona Currie
Andrew Davidson
Brigid Edwards
Pauline Ellison
Graham Evernden
Hargrave Hands
Matthew Hillier
Ronald Lampitt
Carol Lawson
The Royal Horticultural Society (Lindley Library)
Jannat Messenger
Tony Meeuwissen
Karen Murray
Moira McGregor
Andrew McNab
Graham Percy
Marta Sietz
Richard Shirley-Smith
Povl Webb
Sue Windett

Jacket designed by Rita Marshall
Recipe development: Brooke Dojny
    and Melanie Barnard
Recipe consultant: Mimi Errington
Assistant recipe consultant: Anne Higham
Prop stylist: Rebecca Gilles
Food stylist: Nigel Slater
Assistant food stylist: Adrian Barling

Prop credits:

All modern china, glass, and silver courtesy Chinacraft,
556 Oxford Street, Marble Arch, London W1N 9HJ

Rose punch bowl courtesy Asprey, 165-169 New Bond Street,
London W1Y 0AR

A well-stocked pantry is an essential requirement for today's cooking. While undeniably, good quality, fresh ingredients are of the utmost importance, a secondary and equally interesting role is played by prepared foods. Jams, jellies, conserves, marmalades, honeys, oils, vinegars, herbs, and spices fall into this category: They all contain fine seasonal ingredients which, in one way or another, are cooked or blended, then preserved, usually by sealing in glass jars.

For centuries, cooks have known the virtue of judicious seasoning—balancing sweet tastes with savory, bringing out the flavor of meats and fish with complementary herbs, and using oils and vinegars to add character to salads and vegetable dishes. On the following pages we show how seemingly ordinary ingredients can subtly or, in some cases, dramatically, improve the taste of a recipe. Cornish Hens with Honey and Ginger, Cranberry-Port Sauce, and Orange Flower Layer Cake are just a few examples.

In 1699, John Evelyn provided classic advice on the preparation of "sallet dressing" in *Acetaria*: "that the Oyl . . . be smooth, light and pleasant upon the tongue, that the Vinegar be of the best wine vinegar, that the salt be decisive, penetrating, quickening . . . that the mustard (another noble ingredient) be of the best Tewkesberry . . . that the pepper (white or black) be not bruised to too small a dust which, as we cautioned, is very prejudicial." We hope that the recipes in this book will stand such a good test of time.

CRABTREE & EVELYN

TEA

DINNER

COCKTAILS

SUPPER

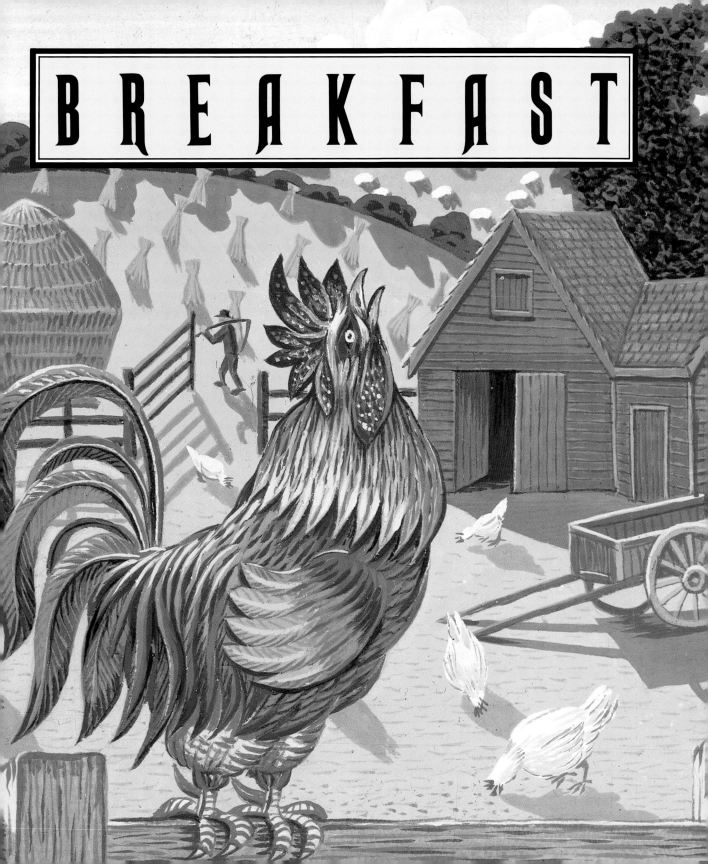

BREAKFAST

HERBAL EXTRACTS

MENU

◆

Sautéed Tomato Cubes

◆

Soft-Boiled Eggs with Herbs

◆

Brioche Jam Toast

OPPOSITE: BRIOCHE JAM TOAST,
SOFT-BOILED EGG WITH HERBS, AND
SAUTÉED TOMATO CUBES

𝒮AUTÉED TOMATO CUBES

3 tablespoons butter
2 to 3 large ripe tomatoes (about 2 pounds), skinned,
    seeded, and cut into cubes
    Pinch sugar
    Salt
    Freshly ground pepper

In a large skillet, melt butter, add tomatoes, and sauté over high heat for 2 minutes, or until they are hot and their juices start to run. Sprinkle with sugar. Season with salt and pepper. Serve warm.

— 4 SERVINGS —

𝒮OFT-BOILED EGGS WITH HERBS

WHEN SELECTING EGGS TO BE SOFT-BOILED AND PEELED, CHOOSE ones that are several days old. With newly laid eggs, chunks of the white often come away with the shell as they are peeled. In addition to the herbs, freshly ground green peppercorns also look attractive on these eggs.

4 large eggs
    Salt
    Freshly ground pepper
10 to 12 sprigs fresh oregano, thyme, sage, rosemary,
    or chervil, with blossoms if possible

Bring a large saucepan of water to a boil over high heat. Gently lower eggs into the saucepan and allow water to return to a simmer. Reduce heat to medium and simmer gently for 3 minutes, stirring eggs carefully 2 to 3 times to center their yolks. Using a slotted spoon, remove eggs from pan and rinse under tepid water to cool them slightly.

Using the back of a spoon, gently crack the shell of each egg all over. Carefully peel away shells and place warm eggs in 4 separate serving bowls. Season eggs with salt and pepper and sprinkle each with 2 to 3 fresh herb sprigs and blossoms.

— 4 SERVINGS —

To skin a tomato simply and quickly, spear the stem end with a fork and dip it into a saucepan of boiling water for several seconds.

Lift it out of the water, slit the skin with a small knife, and peel it off neatly. Remove the seeds by halving the tomato and scooping out the seed cavity with your fingers or a small spoon.

The flowers of kitchen herbs and other edible blooms make delicate decorations for dishes throughout the meal.

Bright nasturtium or soft chive blossoms on green salads, meat, or fish; white basil flowers on sliced tomatoes; and tiny sprigs of rosemary with their mauve flowers on lemon soufflés—all hint at the possibilities of striking combinations.

Brioche Jam Toast

THE BRIOCHE CAN EASILY BE MADE THE DAY BEFORE IT IS NEEDED, OR well in advance and frozen. Cooking jam toast on a ridged griddle creates an attractive pattern, especially if the slices of bread are placed diagonally. The toast can also be made simply by buttering and broiling single slices of brioche and then spreading them with jam.

8   ¼-inch-thick slices brioche (see Appendix), cut
    from center of loaf
⅓   cup raspberry, black currant, or other berry jam
2   tablespoons butter, softened

Spread 4 brioche slices with jam almost to the edges. Top each slice with 1 of the remaining 4 slices. Lightly butter both sides of each sandwich.

Preheat a ridged or flat griddle or frying pan until hot. Place sandwiches diagonally on the griddle and grill for 2 to 3 minutes per side, or until golden brown and crisp. Remove sandwiches from the griddle. Cut each sandwich into 4 equal strips and serve warm.

— 16 JAM TOASTS (4 TO 6 SERVINGS) —

Leftover brioche makes an exalted bread pudding. Sprinkle a few raisins and pieces of chopped citron between each layer of sliced brioche, pour the custard mixture over the top, and bake as indicated. As the pudding emerges from the oven, sprinkle it with a few teaspoons of cinnamon and sugar. Serve warm with cream.

LAZY SUNDAY MORNING

MENU

◆

*T*ANGERINE-
GRAPEFRUIT JUICE

◆

*T*ARRAGON POACHED
EGGS

◆

*C*ANADIAN BACON
SAUTÉED IN BUTTER

◆

*O*AT WAFFLES

OPPOSITE: TANGERINE-GRAPEFRUIT
JUICE AND OAT WAFFLES

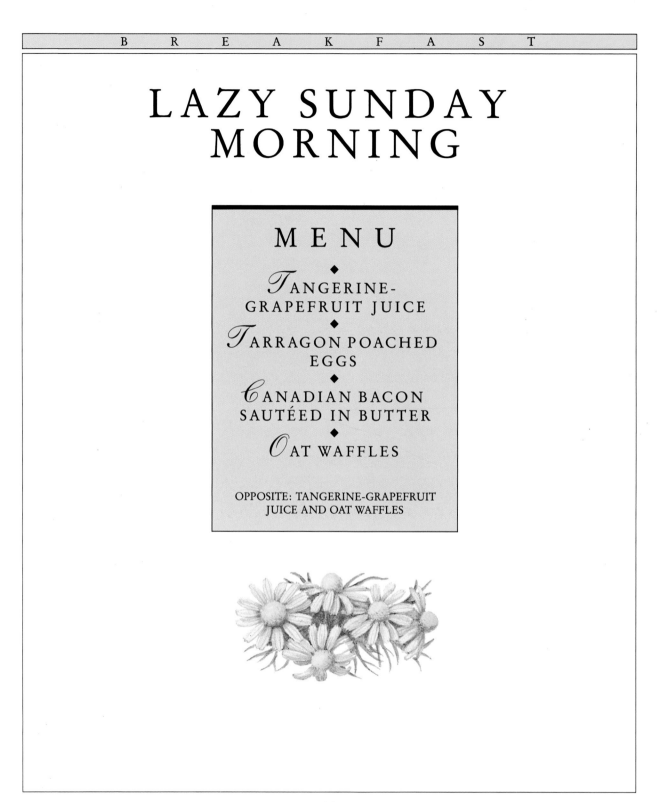

$\mathcal{T}$ANGERINE-GRAPEFRUIT JUICE

6 tangerines, halved
3 medium grapefruits, halved

Using an electric or hand juicer, squeeze juice from tangerines and grapefruit. Combine the juices and chill.

— MAKES ABOUT 4 CUPS —

$\mathcal{T}$ARRAGON POACHED EGGS

3 tablespoons tarragon vinegar
3 sprigs fresh tarragon, or ¼ teaspoon dried tarragon
4 large eggs

TO SERVE
Fresh tarragon sprigs, chopped fresh tarragon, or dried tarragon (optional)

Tarragon's light but pervasive flavor particularly suits eggs, as well as mushrooms, carrots, mild fish, chicken, and veal. It is the flavoring of the classic sauce béarnaise and enhances many salads when added—either chopped or included in the dressing via a tarragon vinegar or tarragon mustard.

Fill a large skillet with 3 cups water, or enough to make a poaching bath at least 1 inch deep. Add vinegar and tarragon. Bring this court bouillon to a simmer over medium-low heat.

Break each egg into a small cup, then carefully slide each into the court bouillon. Simmer gently for about 2 minutes, or until whites are set, spooning the hot liquid over eggs to lightly film yolks. Using a slotted spoon, remove eggs from liquid and sprinkle with fresh or dried tarragon, if desired. Serve warm.

— 4 SERVINGS —

$\mathcal{C}$ANADIAN BACON SAUTÉED IN BUTTER

2 to 3 tablespoons unsalted butter
8 to 12 thin slices Canadian bacon (6 to 8 ounces)

In a large skillet, melt butter over medium heat. Add bacon and sauté until slices are heated through and are lightly browned, about 3 minutes. Do not overcook; this very lean cut of bacon dries out easily. Serve warm.

— 4 SERVINGS —

*O*AT WAFFLES

¾ cup old-fashioned rolled oats (see Note)
3 tablespoons butter, cut into pieces
1¼ cups flour
1 tablespoon sugar
1½ teaspoons baking powder
½ teaspoon baking soda
½ teaspoon salt
2 large eggs
1 cup buttermilk

TO SERVE
Butter
Blueberry or black currant preserves

In a medium saucepan, combine oats with 1¼ cups water. Bring to a simmer over medium heat and cook, stirring frequently, for 3 minutes. Remove from heat and stir butter into hot oatmeal until melted.

Sift flour, sugar, baking powder, baking soda, and salt into a mixing bowl. In another bowl, combine eggs and buttermilk and beat lightly. Stir oatmeal into egg-milk mixture. Add oatmeal mixture to dry ingredients and stir just until well blended; do not overbeat.

Preheat waffle iron until hot.

Cook waffles according to waffle iron manufacturer's directions, using about ¾ cup batter for each 8-inch waffle.

Serve hot with butter and blueberry or black currant preserves.

— MAKES FOUR 8-INCH WAFFLES —

Note: Quick-cooking (but not "instant") oats may be used, but reduce the water to 1 cup and decrease the cooking time to 30 seconds before adding the butter.

If buttermilk is unavailable, ¾ cup thin yogurt mixed with ¼ cup milk may be used instead.

FROSTY MORNING

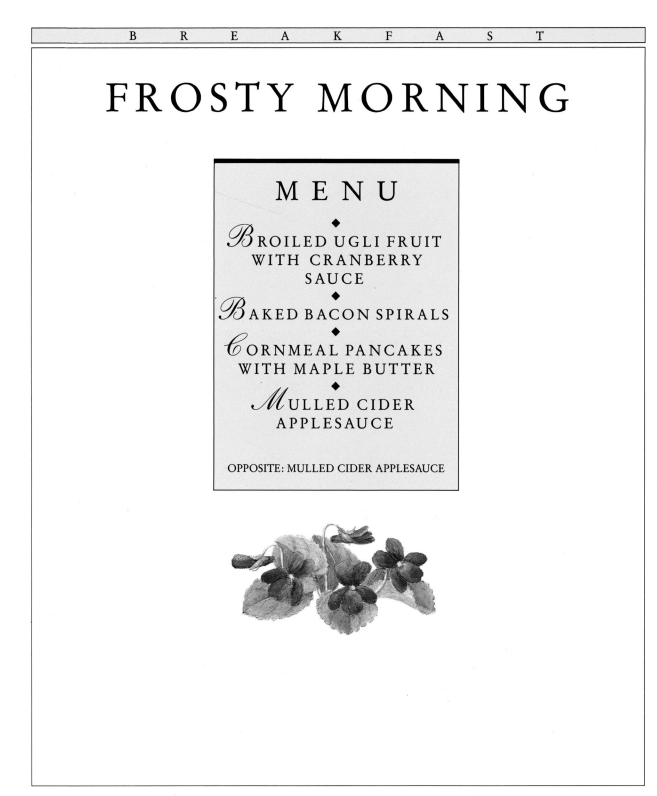

MENU

◆

*B*ROILED UGLI FRUIT
WITH CRANBERRY
SAUCE

◆

*B*AKED BACON SPIRALS

◆

*C*ORNMEAL PANCAKES
WITH MAPLE BUTTER

◆

*M*ULLED CIDER
APPLESAUCE

OPPOSITE: MULLED CIDER APPLESAUCE

BROILED UGLI FRUIT WITH CRANBERRY SAUCE

Tiny uncultivated cranberries, grown principally in Sweden, are known as lingonberries. Their natural flavor has a character often lacking in cultivated berries, and, as they hold their shape during cooking, sauces made with them have a good, firm texture.

USE A GOOD-QUALITY CRANBERRY SAUCE FOR THIS RECIPE. IF UGLI fruit are not available, substitute grapefruit.

2 ripe ugli fruit, halved and seeded
¼ cup cranberry sauce

Preheat broiler.

Loosen ugli fruit halves with a small knife. Place on baking sheet, cut side up, and broil about 4 inches from heat source for 3 minutes.

Remove from broiler and spread each ugli fruit half with 1 tablespoon cranberry sauce. Return fruit to broiler and broil for 3 minutes more, or until the cranberry sauce is hot and bubbly, being careful not to let them burn.

Serve warm.

— 4 SERVINGS —

English Country
CRANBERRY
SAUCE
Our traditional sauce
is cooked in open
copper kettles
using only small wild,
Swedish Cranberries
and sugar.

Made in England

net wt 325g 11.5 OZ

ℬAKED BACON SPIRALS

8   thick slices lean bacon
8   toothpicks

Preheat oven to 400 degrees F.
Roll each bacon slice into a spiral and secure with a toothpick. Arrange spirals on a wire rack over a broiler pan. Place in the center of hot oven and bake for 15 to 18 minutes, or until bacon is crisp and golden brown. Place bacon on paper towels to drain briefly and remove toothpicks.
Serve immediately.

— 4 SERVINGS —

CORNMEAL PANCAKES WITH MAPLE BUTTER

LIGHT, MOIST, AND SLIGHTLY CRUNCHY PANCAKES BALANCE THE sweetness of the maple butter. Even better, they are easy to make, especially if the dry ingredients for the pancakes are sifted into the mixing bowl the night before and the butter for the maple butter is left out to soften overnight.

MAPLE BUTTER
⅔ cup maple syrup
½ cup (1 stick) butter, softened

PANCAKES
⅔ cup cornmeal
⅓ cup flour
2 teaspoons baking powder
½ teaspoon salt
1½ tablespoons sugar
1 large egg
1¼ cups milk
3 tablespoons butter, melted

In a small saucepan, simmer the maple syrup over medium heat 7 to 10 minutes, until reduced to ½ cup. Remove from the heat and let cool to lukewarm. Add softened butter and stir until the mixture is creamy and well blended. Set aside at room temperature.

In a mixing bowl, combine cornmeal, flour, baking powder, salt, and sugar. In another bowl, beat egg lightly, then beat in the milk. Make a well in the center of dry ingredients and slowly stir in milk-egg mixture. Add melted butter and stir until just smooth.

Preheat a greased griddle until a few drops of cold water bounce when splashed on it. Ladle about 3 tablespoons of batter onto the griddle for each pancake, leaving about 3 inches between each to allow for spreading. Cook until bubbles appear on the surfaces, and undersides are golden brown, 2 to 3 minutes. Turn with a spatula and cook until the undersides are lightly browned. Remove pancakes from the griddle and keep them warm while you repeat the process with remaining batter.

Serve pancakes hot, accompanied by maple butter.

— 4 SERVINGS (ABOUT 12 PANCAKES AND 1 CUP MAPLE BUTTER) —

MULLED CIDER APPLESAUCE

THE CONCENTRATED SPICED CIDER GIVES THIS APPLE-sauce a wonderful rich fruitiness. It can be made up to three days ahead and then refrigerated until needed.

1	stick cinnamon, broken in half
3	whole cloves
3	whole allspice berries
1	1-inch strip orange zest
2	cups apple cider
6	to 8 tart apples (about 3 pounds), peeled, cored, and coarsely diced
	Pinch salt
¼	cup firmly packed light brown sugar
¼	to ½ cup granulated sugar
1	tablespoon butter, softened

Place cinnamon, cloves, allspice, and orange zest in a spice bag or in a square of cheesecloth tied securely with string.

In a heavy saucepan, bring cider to a boil over high heat. Add spice bag, reduce heat to medium, and simmer until cider is reduced to ⅔ cup, about 30 minutes. Remove and discard spice bag.

Add apples, salt, and brown sugar to the reduced cider. Cover and simmer over medium-low heat, stirring frequently, until apples become mushy, about 20 minutes.

Taste and add enough granulated sugar to bring mixture to desired sweetness. (The amount of sugar will vary with the sweetness of the apples used.) Add butter and stir until well blended.

Serve warm or lightly chilled.

— MAKES 4 CUPS —

This maple cream sauce, a delicious alternative for the cornmeal pancakes, is rich and smooth and pours like cream. In a small saucepan, heat ⅔ cup maple syrup, ½ cup heavy cream, and 6 tablespoons butter, stirring, until the butter is melted and simmer the mixture over low heat for 10 minutes, or until it is slightly thickened. Let the sauce stand until just warm and stir it well before serving. Makes about 1 cup.

COUNTRY WEEKEND BREAKFAST

MENU

◆

*T*INY FRUITS WITH MINT
AND CRÈME
FRAÎCHE SAUCE

◆

*E*GGS BAKED IN DILL
CRÊPE NESTS

◆

*F*RIZZLED HAM STRIPS
ON WATERCRESS

◆

*M*ARMALADE MUFFINS

OPPOSITE: MARMALADE MUFFINS,
TINY FRUITS WITH MINT AND CRÈME
FRAÎCHE SAUCE, EGGS BAKED IN
DILL CRÊPE NESTS, AND FRIZZLED
HAM STRIPS ON WATERCRESS

*T*INY FRUITS WITH MINT AND CRÈME FRAÎCHE SAUCE

To make crème fraîche, *mix 1 cup sour cream with 1 to 2 cups fresh heavy cream (do not use cream that has been "ultra-pasteurized" to extend its shelf life).*

Let the mixture stand, unrefrigerated, for several hours, or until it is thickened. Cover and refrigerate.

1 cup *crème fraîche* (see Note)
2 tablespoons heavy cream
2 tablespoons chopped fresh mint leaves, or 1 teaspoon dried mint
3 to 4 tablespoons powdered sugar
2 cups berries or grapes, preferably a mixture of raspberries, strawberries, blueberries, and red and green grapes

TO SERVE
Fresh mint sprigs

In a small mixing bowl, combine *crème fraîche*, heavy cream, chopped mint, and powdered sugar. If mixture is too thick, add more heavy cream. If it's not sweet enough, add more powdered sugar. Spoon into a decorative serving dish and set aside.

Combine fruit in a large bowl and mix. Divide between 4 individual serving plates or shallow dishes. Garnish with mint sprigs.

Spoon a mound of the *crème fraîche* sauce onto each serving plate next to the fruit and pass remaining sauce at the table.

— 4 SERVINGS —

Note: If *crème fraîche* is unavailable, sour cream can be substituted, and the heavy cream, which is added to thin the *crème fraîche* slightly, can be omitted.

Marmalade Muffins

Any thick jam or preserve can be used in place of the marmalade, but these are especially pretty when a variety of colorful
marmalades and preserves fills the muffins.

1¾ cups flour
3   teaspoons baking powder
½   teaspoon baking soda
2   tablespoons granulated sugar
2   tablespoons light brown sugar
½   teaspoon salt
1   large egg
1   cup milk
4   tablespoons butter, melted and cooled
1   tablespoon grated orange zest
6   tablespoons orange or lemon marmalade or other
    fruit preserve

Preheat oven to 400 degrees F.

In a large mixing bowl, sift flour, baking powder, baking soda,
granulated sugar, brown sugar, and salt together. In a separate bowl beat
egg lightly, then beat in the milk. Mix butter and orange zest into egg-
milk mixture. Make a well in the center of dry ingredients and add liquid
mixture all at once. Using a large wooden spoon, stir batter with 10 to 15
swift strokes, or until ingredients are just combined. Do not overmix;
batter should remain slightly lumpy.

Spoon about 2 tablespoons of batter into the bottom of each of 12
generously greased muffin tins. Add 1½ teaspoons marmalade to each
muffin tin. Then add enough additional batter to fill each ¾ full.

Bake in the center of oven for 18 to 20 minutes, or until muffins are
golden brown and a toothpick inserted into centers comes out free of
batter. Turn out of muffin tins onto a wire rack to cool slightly. Serve
warm.

— MAKES 12 MUFFINS —

Marmalade, as much a part of the British break-fast ritual as a copy of The Times, *takes its name from* marmelo, *Portuguese for "quince" (because marmalades before the eighteenth century were usually sweet quince pastes). Today, they are almost always made from citrus fruits in a wide variety of combinations, and even the simplest British orange marmalades range from lightly flavored ones made with sweet oranges and finely sliced rinds to dark, sharper-tasting varieties made with bitter, or Seville, oranges.*

EGGS BAKED IN DILL CRÊPE NESTS

CRÊPES MAY BE MADE IN ADVANCE AND KEPT IN THE REFRIGERATOR overnight or frozen. To store, stack them between pieces of waxed paper, place in a plastic bag, and refrigerate.

CRÊPES
½ cup flour
⅛ teaspoon salt
⅛ teaspoon freshly ground white pepper
½ cup milk
1 whole large egg
1 large egg yolk
1 tablespoon chopped fresh dill, or 1 teaspoon dried
1½ tablespoons butter, melted

BAKED EGGS
8 large eggs
Salt
Freshly ground black pepper
3 tablespoons butter, melted
8 sprigs fresh dill

In a large mixing bowl, combine flour, salt, and white pepper. Make a well in the center of dry ingredients. Combine milk with 3 tablespoons water and stir gradually into dry ingredients. In a small bowl, beat whole egg and yolk together lightly. Add eggs to batter, along with the dill and butter. Stir just until ingredients are blended. Let batter rest for 1 to 2 hours before making crêpes.

To prepare crêpes, heat a lightly greased 5- to 5½-inch crêpe pan over medium-high heat until beads of water sizzle when dropped on the surface. Stir crêpe batter, then ladle 1½ to 2 tablespoons batter into the pan and swirl to coat surface completely. Let cook until bottom of crêpe is lightly browned, 30 to 45 seconds. Turn with a spatula and brown the other side for 15 to 20 seconds. Turn onto a wire rack to cool, then stack on a plate between layers of waxed paper. Continue in this manner until all crêpe batter is used, adding more butter to the pan as needed.

Preheat oven to 350 degrees F.

Ease 1 crêpe into each of 8 generously buttered, standard-size muffin tins, gently ruffling edges. Bake in the center of the oven 8 minutes. Break an egg into each crêpe cup and season each with salt and black pepper. Bake for 7 to 9 minutes, or until whites of eggs are set but yolks are still runny. Remove from the oven and, using both hands, carefully lift crêpe cups from muffin tins onto serving plates. Drizzle about 1 teaspoon butter over each egg and garnish with dill. Serve immediately.

— 4 TO 8 SERVINGS (14 TO 16 CRÊPES) —

Simple crêpes–the makings of Pancake Day, or Shrove Tuesday, in Britain–were once the final extravagance before Lent. Sprinkle sugar and enough fresh lemon juice on each crêpe to sharpen the taste and roll the crêpe up. Arrange on a warm serving plate with lemon wedges and the leaves and lemon-colored blossoms of primroses, if available.

FRIZZLED HAM STRIPS ON WATERCRESS

6   ounces lightly smoked ham, cut into ⅛-inch-thick
    slices
2   tablespoons unsalted butter
2   teaspoons black currant or raspberry vinegar
1   large bunch watercress, stems removed
    Salt
    Freshly ground pepper

Cut ham slices into 1½- by ¼-inch strips. In a medium skillet, melt 1 tablespoon of the butter. Add ham strips and sauté over medium-high heat, tossing gently, for 3 to 4 minutes, or until golden brown, slightly curled, and crispy. Remove ham strips and keep them warm.

Add vinegar to the skillet and swirl to deglaze. Add remaining 1 tablespoon butter and melt. Add watercress and sauté over medium-high heat, tossing gently, for 30 to 45 seconds, or until it begins to wilt. Remove from heat, season with salt and pepper, and toss.

Arrange watercress on a warmed serving platter. Top with ham strips and serve immediately.

— 4 SERVINGS —

In summer, substitute sorrel for watercress. Tear tender sorrel leaves into roughly inch-square pieces before adding them to the juices in the pan, preferably a non-reactive pan to prevent the leaves from darkening.

FOR THE ARMCHAIR CAMPER

MENU

◆

*S*TRAWBERRIES
WITH STRAWBERRY
VINEGAR

◆

*P*OTATO PANCAKES
WITH PEPPER RELISH

◆

*H*OME-SMOKED TROUT
WITH ROSEMARY

OPPOSITE: HOME-SMOKED TROUT WITH
ROSEMARY

The Rainbow Trout

Salmo gairdneri irideus

Salmo gairdneri irideus — male in the spawning season

STRAWBERRIES WITH STRAWBERRY VINEGAR

THE BERRIES MUST BE UTTERLY RIPE AND VERY SWEET; THEIR FLAVOR and aroma are then heightened by the vinegar. They are also best served at room temperature, so that their fragrance is released.

1   pint ripe strawberries with stems
2   to 3 tablespoons strawberry vinegar

Shortly before serving, rinse berries briefly in cold water, drain, and pat dry with paper towels.

 Arrange berries in a shallow serving bowl. Sprinkle with the vinegar and serve. No utensils are needed; pick up berries by the stems to eat.

— 4 SERVINGS —

Line the serving bowl with strawberry leaves, if available, to make a fresh background for the berries. Then sprinkle a few drops of rosewater over the berries just before serving. Strawberries and roses belong to the same botanical family, and their aromas complement each other wonderfully.

HOME-SMOKED TROUT
WITH ROSEMARY

THE TROUT IS SOAKED IN BRINE FOR A DAY BEFORE IT IS COOKED AND should be smoked in a covered barbecue grill. Serve the trout warm, soon after grilling.

- 2 whole 8- to 10-ounce fresh trout
- ¼ cup coarse salt
  Hickory chips or other wood chips for barbecuing
- 2 sprigs fresh rosemary

ROSEMARY BUTTER
- 3 tablespoons unsalted butter, softened
- 1 teaspoon minced fresh rosemary, or ½ teaspoon dried rosemary

To soak, rinse trout thoroughly in water, place in a 3-quart enamel or other non-reactive pan, and add salt and 2 quarts water. The fish should be completely covered with brine. Cover and refrigerate for 24 hours.

Place 2 to 3 handfuls of hickory chips in a basin of cold water and soak for 30 minutes. About an hour before serving the fish, build an indirect barbecue fire by placing the charcoal to one side of the kettle of the barbecue grill. When the charcoal becomes gray-white, drain the hickory chips and toss them onto the fire. Oil the grill, cover the kettle, and leave the fire for 5 to 10 minutes.

Remove trout from brine, drain, and rinse under cold water. Using a sharp knife, remove heads and slit down the center along back bone on inside to butterfly each trout.

Place trout, skin side down, on the grill away from the hot coals so that they cook over indirect heat. Lay fresh rosemary sprigs on the fish. Cover barbecue grill and let trout smoke for about 40 minutes, or until the flesh is cooked through.

In a small bowl, combine butter and minced rosemary and beat until blended.

Remove trout from the grill. Cut each in half lengthwise and serve topped with dollops of the rosemary butter.

— 4 BREAKFAST SERVINGS —

As a lunch or dinner dish, this trout is excellent served with a piquant horseradish sauce made by stirring 2 to 4 tablespoons Crabtree & Evelyn Horseradish Sauce into ½ cup sour cream or crème fraîche.

POTATO PANCAKES WITH
CHILI PEPPER RELISH

Potato pancakes are delicious served with poached eggs. Drain the eggs very well, place one on each pancake, and spoon the relish on top. The relish is also a fine accompaniment to scrambled or fried eggs and a colorful filling for an omelet.

IF ANY OF THE CHILI PEPPERS ARE UNAVAILABLE, SUBSTITUTE HALF A small green, yellow, or red bell pepper for the chili pepper of the same color in the recipe. The relish should be brightly colored and also have some bite, so use the Tabasco sauce to strike the right balance of hotness, depending on the heat of the chili peppers. Also, the relish can be made the night before and reheated at the last minute.

CHILI PEPPER RELISH

1   tablespoon vegetable oil
1   jalapeño pepper, cored, seeded, and minced
1   small yellow chili pepper, cored, seeded, and minced
1   small mild red chili pepper, cored, seeded, and minced
2   tablespoons thinly sliced green onion
2   tablespoons white-wine vinegar
    Several drops Tabasco or other hot pepper sauce (optional)
    Salt
    Freshly ground black pepper

POTATO PANCAKES

1   large egg
1   tablespoon flour
¼   teaspoon salt
    Pinch freshly ground black pepper
2   large all-purpose potatoes (about 1 pound), peeled, coarsely grated, and set aside in a bowl of cold water
1   to 2 tablespoons butter
1   tablespoon vegetable oil

To prepare the relish, heat oil in a medium skillet. Add jalapeño, yellow and red chili peppers, and green onion and sauté over medium heat for about 3 minutes. Turn mixture into a small bowl. Return skillet to the heat, add vinegar, and swirl for 30 seconds over medium heat to deglaze skillet. Pour vinegar into pepper-onion mixture. Let cool slightly and taste. Season with Tabasco, if desired, salt, and pepper. Set aside.

In a mixing bowl, combine egg, flour, salt, and black pepper and beat together lightly. Drain potatoes in a colander and pat dry with paper towels. Add potatoes to egg batter and toss until well coated.

Preheat oven to 200 degrees F.

In a large skillet, heat half the butter and half the oil over medium-high heat until hot. Spoon about ¼ of potato mixture into the skillet and flatten into a 5-inch pancake. Spoon another ¼ of the mixture into the skillet, allowing a few inches between the two pancakes, and flatten. Cook over medium heat for 5 minutes, or until the bottoms are lightly browned. Carefully turn the pancakes with a spatula and cook until the other sides are lightly browned and pancakes are cooked through. Transfer pancakes to a baking sheet and place in the oven to keep warm. Use remaining batter and remaining butter and oil to make two more 5-inch potato pancakes in the same manner.

Spoon a little relish on each pancake and serve.

— 4 SERVINGS —

For a fine accompaniment to roasted meats and fish dishes, vary this potato pancakes recipe by using only 1 large potato and substituting an equal quantity of raw turnip for the second potato. Treat both vegetables in the same way as the potatoes in the recipe, but make the mixture into 8 smaller pancakes instead of the 4 suggested.

BRUNCH

INTERMEZZO

M E N U

◆

*C*RANBERRY-ORANGE
JUICE

◆

*S*CRAMBLED EGGS WITH
CHEDDAR AND CHIVES

◆

*S*IMPLE SAUSAGE
PATTIES

◆

*P*EPPERY CORNSTICKS

◆

*A*ROMATIC PEARS

OPPOSITE: AROMATIC PEAR AND
CRANBERRY-ORANGE JUICE

CRANBERRY-ORANGE JUICE

USE THE SWEETEST, RIPEST ORANGES AVAILABLE.

6 cups cranberry juice
¾ cup freshly squeezed orange juice

TO SERVE
6 orange slices

Combine cranberry and orange juices in a pitcher and stir to blend well. Chill until serving time.

Pour into 6 tall glasses filled with ice cubes. Garnish the rim of each glass with an orange slice.

— 6 SERVINGS —

SCRAMBLED EGGS
WITH CHEDDAR AND CHIVES

THE CHEESE THAT FALLS ON THE SCRAMBLED EGGS MELTS ON THE WAY to the table; the rest stays whole, in feathery strands over the top. Serve the eggs in a warm serving dish or from the skillet in which they have cooked and pass the salt separately, as the Cheddar may well have added enough saltiness to the dish.

12 large eggs
⅓ cup milk
2 teaspoons whole-grain mustard
3 tablespoons unsalted butter
1½ cups grated sharp Cheddar cheese

2 to 3 tablespoons snipped chives or finely sliced green onion tops
Freshly ground pepper
Salt (optional)

In a large mixing bowl, combine eggs, milk, and mustard and beat together lightly.

In a large skillet, melt butter. Add eggs and cook over low heat, stirring almost constantly, until they have formed into a creamy mass but are not yet completely set; eggs should not be dry.

Carefully slide the eggs onto a warm serving platter, or finish preparing and serve from skillet. Sprinkle eggs with grated cheese. Scatter chives over cheese and top with a generous grind of pepper. Serve immediately.

— 6 SERVINGS —

It is worth seeking out aged farmhouse Cheddar, as its deep nutty flavor will season more assertively than the milder, young Cheddars that are more generally available.

40

PEPPERY CORNSTICKS

HEAVY CAST-IRON CORNSTICK PANS ARE MOLDED TO MAKE MUFFINS IN the shape of ears of corn; they should be greased with bacon fat, oil, or margarine—never butter.

Bacon fat or margarine, melted
1 cup cornmeal
1 cup flour
2 tablespoons sugar
4 teaspoons baking powder
½ teaspoon salt
½ teaspoon freshly ground white pepper
1 large egg
1 cup milk
4 tablespoons unsalted butter, melted

Preheat oven to 425 degrees F.

Brush 14 cornstick molds lightly with bacon fat and heat in the oven while making batter.

Sift cornmeal, flour, sugar, baking powder, salt, and pepper into a large mixing bowl. In a small bowl, beat the egg lightly, then beat in the milk and butter. Make a well in the center of dry ingredients, add egg-milk mixture, and stir just to combine.

Remove hot cornstick molds from oven and fill each with about 2 tablespoons batter, spreading batter out evenly so that it fills each corn shape completely.

Return molds to hot oven and bake for 9 to 11 minutes, or until cornsticks are cooked through and lightly browned on top. (This batter can also be cooked in 12 standard prepared muffin tins, at 400 degrees F. for about 20 minutes.) Lift cornsticks out of molds with a small knife, place in a napkin-lined basket, and serve warm.

— 14 CORNSTICKS —

Crumbled cornsticks or cornbread can be used in place of any other bread (usually white) to make an excellent stuffing for chicken or turkey.

$\mathscr{S}$IMPLE SAUSAGE PATTIES

SAGE AND PEPPER ARE TRADITIONAL FLAVORINGS OF ENGLISH FARM-house sausage meat. If this is prepared a day ahead, the flavors mingle beautifully.

2 pounds boneless lean pork, cut into 1½-inch cubes
1 small clove garlic
1¼ teaspoons coarse salt
2 teaspoons minced fresh sage leaves, or ¾ teaspoon dried sage
2 teaspoons coarsely ground black pepper
¼ teaspoon cayenne
  Pinch ground nutmeg
1 to 2 tablespoons butter

For variety, substitute ¾ teaspoon dried oregano or 1 teaspoon fennel seeds for the sage.

Freeze pork in a single layer on a baking sheet for about 45 minutes, or until meat is partially frozen. Working with a quarter of the pork at a time, pulse the meat in a food processor until coarsely ground and crumbly.

Finely chop and mash garlic and salt together on a cutting board to form a paste. In a large mixing bowl, combine garlic-salt paste, sage, black pepper, cayenne, and nutmeg. Add ground meat to the spice mixture and, using fingertips or a wooden spoon, combine the pork thoroughly with seasonings. Chill in the refrigerator for at least 1 hour to allow flavors to blend and intensify.

To verify seasoning, fry a small piece of the sausage mixture well before serving time and taste. Correct seasoning if necessary.

Shortly before serving, shape meat into 2½-inch patties. Melt butter in a large skillet over medium-low heat. Add several patties and cook for 4 to 6 minutes on each side, or until patties are crisp and browned on the outside and no longer pink inside. Place patties on a warm serving platter and keep them warm while you prepare remaining patties. Serve hot.

— 6 SERVINGS (ABOUT 12 PATTIES) —

Aromatic Pears

THE FRAGRANCE OF THIS DISH SHARPENS THE APPETITE FOR THE warmer flavors of fall and winter cooking. The pears are most elegantly served at room temperature or chilled but are also excellent eaten warm for supper on a cold night.

Seckel pears are a small, firm, brown-skinned variety. Six Bosc or other firm-fleshed, standard-size pears may be used instead. Larger pears may need 10 to 15 minutes more cooking, unless they are very ripe.

1 lemon	
1 cup dry white wine	
5 tablespoons sugar	TO SERVE
½ vanilla bean	1 cup heavy cream, whipped
1 stick cinnamon	to soft peaks and chilled
2 whole cloves	
⅛ teaspoon ground ginger	
12 Seckel pears (2 to 2½ pounds)	

Grate zest from the lemon with a sharp hand grater and set aside. Halve lemon, extract 1 tablespoon juice, and set lemon halves and juice aside.

In a large, heavy saucepan, combine lemon zest, wine, sugar, vanilla bean, cinnamon stick, cloves, ginger, and 2 cups water. Bring mixture to a boil over medium-high heat. Lower heat to medium-low and simmer syrup for about 5 minutes.

Meanwhile peel pears with a vegetable peeler, leaving stems on. Rub the surfaces of the pears with the cut side of a lemon half to prevent them from darkening. Poach pears in the syrup until tender, 10 to 20 minutes, stirring and turning pears 2 or 3 times so that they cook evenly. (Pears are cooked when their flesh can be pierced easily with the tip of a knife.) Remove saucepan from heat and let pears cool in syrup for about 10 minutes.

Using a slotted spoon, remove pears from syrup and arrange them, stem ends up, in a shallow serving dish. Return syrup to a boil over high heat until reduced to 1½ cups. Stir in lemon juice. Remove syrup from heat and let cool to lukewarm.

Carefully strain syrup over pears. To serve, pass pears accompanied by whipped cream in a separate bowl.

— 6 SERVINGS —

For a gingery, robust syrup for these pears, replace the sugar and ground ginger with 5 tablespoons Crabtree & Evelyn Honey & Ginger Sauce. Its warm spiciness sets off the coolness of the pears.

FOREIGN EXCHANGE

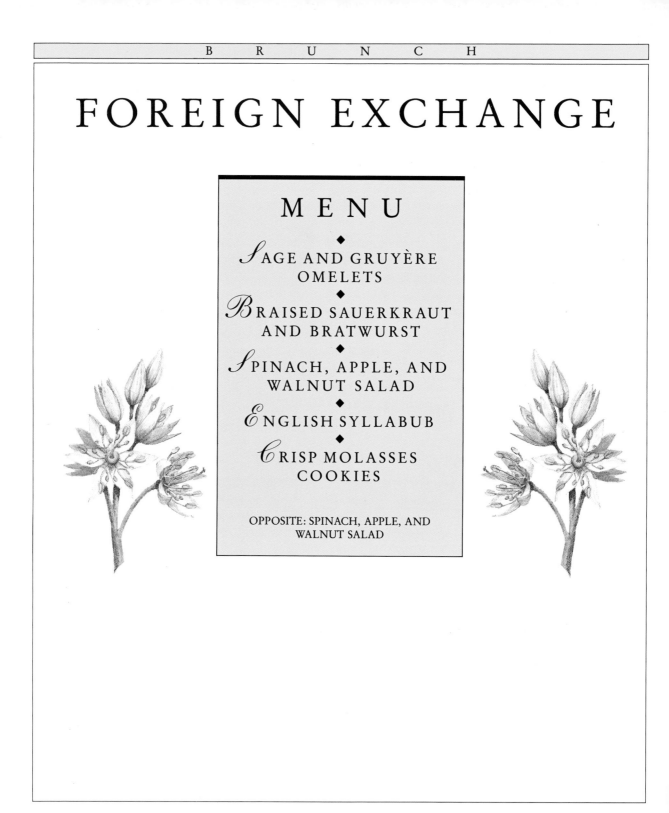

MENU

◆

*S*AGE AND GRUYÈRE
OMELETS

◆

*B*RAISED SAUERKRAUT
AND BRATWURST

◆

*S*PINACH, APPLE, AND
WALNUT SALAD

◆

*E*NGLISH SYLLABUB

◆

*C*RISP MOLASSES
COOKIES

OPPOSITE: SPINACH, APPLE, AND
WALNUT SALAD

$\mathscr{S}$AGE AND GRUYÈRE OMELETS

EACH OMELET TAKES LESS THAN A MINUTE TO MAKE. THE QUANTITIES can be adjusted to increase or decrease the number of servings, but, as omelets should be eaten immediately, it is usually impractical to cook them for more than four people at a time.

8 large eggs	2 tablespoons unsalted butter
2 teaspoons chopped fresh sage leaves, or ¾ teaspoon dried sage	½ cup grated Gruyère cheese
Salt	TO SERVE
Freshly ground pepper	4 sprigs fresh sage (optional)

Crack eggs into a large mixing bowl. Add sage, salt, and pepper and beat lightly with a fork.

In a 7- or 8-inch omelet pan or heavy skillet, melt ½ tablespoon of the butter over medium-high heat until foamy. When foam subsides, add one fourth of the egg mixture and swirl pan to distribute evenly. As eggs begin to set, lift edge gently with a fork or spatula and tilt pan to allow uncooked eggs to run underneath. When eggs are nearly set but still very moist, after about 40 seconds, sprinkle a quarter of the grated cheese across the center of the omelet. Gently fold omelet in half with a spatula and slide it onto a warm serving plate.

Repeat process with remaining eggs and cheese to make three more individual omelets.

Garnish each omelet with a sprig of fresh sage, if desired, and serve immediately.

— 4 SERVINGS —

With its distinctive flavor and creamy texture when melted, Gruyère is one of the best cooking cheeses. Try it folded into scrambled eggs (topped with fried croutons), on pasta, in cheese bread puddings, in deep-fried cheese squares and fritters, and in combination with freshly grated Parmesan in soufflés, gratin toppings, and cream sauces. And, to appreciate Gruyère at its best when eaten with fruit, cut the cheese into very thin slices with a slotted cheese slicer.

Spinach, Apple, and Walnut Salad

¼ cup broken or coarsely chopped walnuts

DRESSING
¼ cup walnut oil
¼ cup vegetable oil
2 tablespoons black currant wine vinegar or other fruit-flavored wine vinegar
   Salt
   Freshly ground pepper

TO SERVE
10 ounces fresh spinach leaves (about 4 cups), washed, dried, and stems removed
1 red Delicious apple, cored but not peeled
1 teaspoon lemon juice

Preheat oven to 350 degrees F.

Spread walnuts on a baking sheet and bake until lightly toasted and fragrant, 5 to 8 minutes, watching carefully to prevent burning. Turn the oven off but keep walnuts warm in the oven until needed.

In a small bowl, whisk together walnut oil, vegetable oil, and vinegar. Season with salt and pepper and whisk until blended.

Tear spinach leaves into bite-size pieces and place in a large salad bowl. Slice apple as thinly as possible, sprinkle with lemon juice, and add to salad bowl. Add vinaigrette and toss to coat spinach and apples well. Divide salad among 4 salad plates and sprinkle each portion with toasted nuts.

— 4 SERVINGS —

When spinach leaves are tender and small, make the salad into a centerpiece for your table. Snip away the stems and arrange the leaves, stem ends down, in a shallow salad bowl in concentric circles so that the salad has the look of a huge flower. Mix the apple slices with the dressing and spoon the mixture into the center of the leaves. Sprinkle the rest of the dressing over the spinach leaves, and the nuts on top of the apples.

$\mathscr{B}$RAISED SAUERKRAUT
AND BRATWURST

THIS DISH CAN BE PREPARED AHEAD TO THE POINT WHERE THE SAU-
sages are added to the sauerkraut. Other mild sausage meat may be used
instead of bratwurst, in which case omit the bacon fat for sautéeing.

The braised sauerkraut, without sausage added, makes a fine accompaniment for roast duck or pheasant.

4 bratwurst sausages (about ¾ pound)
2 tablespoons melted bacon fat
1 small onion, chopped (about ¼ cup)
1 pound sauerkraut, rinsed and drained well
¼ cup apple cider or apple juice
¼ cup dry white wine
1 bay leaf
4 whole juniper berries
¼ teaspoon dried thyme
    Freshly ground pepper
    Salt (optional)

In a large, heavy skillet, sauté sausages in bacon fat until golden brown
and just heated through, about 10 minutes. Remove from skillet and set
aside. Pour off all but 1 tablespoon pan drippings.

Add onions to skillet and sauté over medium heat until softened and
translucent, about 4 minutes. Stir in sauerkraut, cider, and wine. Break
bay leaf in half and add to skillet. Crush juniper berries slightly and add,
along with thyme. Season generously with pepper and stir until well
mixed. Cover skillet and simmer over medium-low heat for about 15
minutes. Taste sauerkraut for seasoning and add salt, if desired. Arrange
sausages on top of sauerkraut. Partially cover skillet and simmer over
medium-low heat for 5 to 10 minutes longer, or until sausages are heated
through. Discard bay leaf halves.

Transfer to a platter or distribute among individual plates and serve
immediately.

— 4 SERVINGS —

ENGLISH SYLLABUB

THIS IRRESISTIBLE DESSERT SHOULD BE MADE THE DAY IT IS TO BE eaten. Sherry is often used in place of the white wine, and either version makes a superb filling for the Molasses-Rum Lace Wafers on page 227.

2   lemons
⅓   cup medium-dry white wine
1   to 2 tablespoons brandy
⅓   cup sugar
1   cup heavy cream

FOR DECORATION
4   sprigs fresh mint, if desired

Strain the mixture through a sieve into a larger bowl and discard the zest. With an electric mixer set at low, beat the lemon mixture while slowly pouring in the cream and continue beating for 2 to 3 minutes, or until the syllabub is just thick enough to hold the marks of the beater. Divide the syllabub among 4 bowls or glasses, cover with plastic wrap, and refrigerate.

Before serving, decorate with the mint.

— SERVES 4 —

This perennial English favorite combines the creamiest of textures with a sharp, refreshing taste. Syllabub has been known for centuries and, in its simplest form, was made by directing milk straight from the cow's udder into a bowl of cider or wine.

$\mathcal{M}$OLASSES COOKIES

THESE SPICY, SLIGHTLY SOFT COOKIES ARE DELICIOUS WITH A LIGHT mousse, ice cream, or fresh fruit.

2 cups flour
½ teaspoon baking soda
½ teaspoon salt
1 teaspoon ground cinnamon
½ teaspoon ground ginger
¾ cup sugar
½ cup unsalted butter, softened
½ cup molasses
1 large egg, lightly beaten
1 tablespoon grated fresh gingerroot

When measuring molasses, lightly butter or oil the measuring cup; the molasses then slides from the cup without sticking to the sides. This also increases the accuracy of the measuring.

Sift flour, baking soda, salt, cinnamon, and ground ginger together on a sheet of waxed paper and set aside.

In a large mixing bowl, cream together ½ cup of the sugar and the butter until light and fluffy. Add molasses, egg, and gingerroot and beat until light. Gradually add the flour, stirring until well blended. Cover dough and chill for at least 1 hour or overnight.

Preheat oven to 350 degrees F.

Form dough into 1-inch balls, rolling them between the palms until smooth and round. Spread remaining ¼ cup sugar on waxed paper and roll each ball of dough in sugar. Place dough balls 2 inches apart on greased baking sheets. Bake in the center of hot oven until tops are rounded and crinkled and cookies are just beginning to color, about 12 to 14 minutes. Remove from the oven and transfer to wire racks to cool. Store in a tightly covered container.

— MAKES ABOUT 32 COOKIES —

COUNTRY PURSUITS

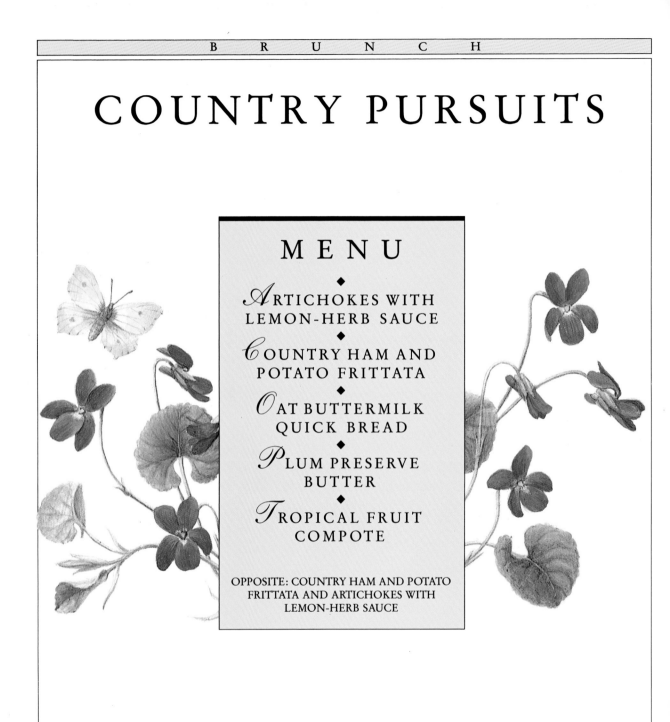

M E N U

◆

ARTICHOKES WITH
LEMON-HERB SAUCE

◆

COUNTRY HAM AND
POTATO FRITTATA

◆

OAT BUTTERMILK
QUICK BREAD

◆

PLUM PRESERVE
BUTTER

◆

TROPICAL FRUIT
COMPOTE

OPPOSITE: COUNTRY HAM AND POTATO
FRITTATA AND ARTICHOKES WITH
LEMON-HERB SAUCE

ARTICHOKES WITH LEMON-HERB SAUCE

THE ARTICHOKES MAY BE SERVED WARM, OR THEY MAY BE CHILLED IN the refrigerator for up to 8 hours and eaten cold. The sauce can be made up to 2 days ahead and chilled. Either way, fill the artichokes just before serving.

6 whole medium artichokes
½ lemon
½ teaspoon salt

LEMON-HERB SAUCE
1 large egg
2 teaspoons whole-grain mustard
1 to 1½ tablespoons fresh lemon juice
¾ cup vegetable oil
1 teaspoon grated lemon zest
2 tablespoons finely chopped fresh chives

1 tablespoon finely chopped fresh parsley
Salt
Freshly ground pepper

TO SERVE
Lemon wedges

This light sauce is also excellent poured over tiny boiled new potatoes, green beans, or broccoli.

Trim artichokes, cutting off stems at base, removing tough outer leaves, and using kitchen scissors to cut off spiky points of remaining leaves. Rinse under cold water. Rub cut side of lemon over cut edges of artichokes to prevent darkening.

Set artichokes, stem ends down, in a very large saucepan or stockpot. Slowly add 2 inches of water. Add salt and squeeze remaining juice from lemon half into pan. Cover and bring liquid to a boil. Lower heat to medium-low and steam artichokes, covered, for 25 to 30 minutes, or until stems are tender enough to be pierced easily with a knife. Remove artichokes from the pan with tongs and invert on a flat surface to drain. Let drain until cool enough to handle.

Meanwhile prepare sauce. Break egg into food processor or large mixing bowl. Add mustard and lemon juice and process or beat until blended. With processor motor running, dribble in oil through feed tube in a slow steady stream. If preparing by hand, add a few drops of oil at a time, whisking vigorously between each addition, until mixture begins to thicken. Add remaining oil in a slow steady stream, whisking constantly until all oil is incorporated. Scrape down sides of processor or bowl with a spatula, add lemon zest, chives, and parsley. Season to taste with salt and pepper and blend well.

Gently pull apart inner leaves of each artichoke until you see the tender, pale green, cone-shaped leaves at center. Remove and discard these inner leaves. Using a small spoon, carefully scrape out and discard the fuzzy choke at the center of each artichoke. Arrange artichokes on a large serving platter. Spoon 2 to 3 tablespoons of sauce into the center cavity of each artichoke. Arrange lemon wedges around artichokes. Place any remaining sauce in a sauceboat and serve separately.

— 6 SERVINGS —

$\mathcal{O}$AT BUTTERMILK QUICK BREAD

THIS BREAD IS AN EXCELLENT VEHICLE FOR GOOD PRESERVES. IT CAN be frozen or made up to three days before it is needed and stored in the refrigerator; it is more easily cut when cold. To serve, slice it into ½-inch-thick slices and arrange in a basket. Cover well and let the bread come to room temperature. Eat it with Plum Preserve Butter (page 57) or plain butter and a selection of preserves.

1 cup all-purpose flour	¼ cup honey
¾ cup whole-wheat flour	1½ cups buttermilk
1 teaspoon baking powder	¼ cup butter, melted and cooled
½ teaspoon baking soda	¾ cup regular (not instant)
½ teaspoon salt	rolled oats
1 large egg	½ cup currants

If the honey has hardened in the cupboard or refrigerator, stand the jar, uncovered, in a saucepan of barely simmering water for 15 to 20 minutes, or until the honey softens. Or leave it in a warm place overnight.

Preheat oven to 350 degrees F.

Sift all-purpose flour, whole-wheat flour, baking powder, baking soda, and salt together onto a sheet of waxed paper. In a large mixing bowl, combine egg, honey, buttermilk, and butter and beat together lightly. Stir in oats and currants. Add flour mixture all at once and stir batter with a few swift strokes until just blended; do not overmix. (Batter will be quite stiff.)

Line the bottom of a greased medium loaf pan with parchment or waxed paper. Pour batter into the pan and smooth top with a spatula. Bake in the center of hot oven for 60 to 65 minutes, or until top of bread is deep golden brown and a toothpick inserted into the center comes out clean. Let cool in the pan for 10 minutes, then turn out onto a wire rack, removing parchment from bread, and let cool completely. Wrap in plastic wrap or aluminum foil and refrigerate until well chilled.

— MAKES 1 LOAF (ABOUT 14 SLICES) —

COUNTRY HAM AND POTATO FRITTATA

THE COMBINATION OF THE HAM SQUARES AND POTATO SLICES WITH the parsley and eggs gives this dish a colorful mosaic pattern when cut. For brunch, serve it hot, spooned out of the dish; or warm, cut into squares. Cold, the frittata is excellent picnic fare.

2   medium boiling potatoes, unpeeled
10 large eggs
¼   cup chopped fresh parsley
3   tablespoons olive oil
1   small onion, peeled and thinly sliced
¼   pound thinly sliced country ham, cut into 1-inch squares
½   cup grated Parmesan or Gruyère cheese
    Freshly ground pepper to taste

Place potatoes in a saucepan of lightly salted boiling water and boil until just tender. Drain and set aside to cool. Break eggs into a large mixing bowl and beat until well mixed but not frothy. Stir in parsley.

Preheat oven to 400 degrees F.

Pour oil into a 2-quart square or oval baking dish and swirl to coat bottom of dish evenly. Scatter onion slices evenly over bottom of dish. Place in hot oven for 10 minutes, or until onion slices are softened and just beginning to brown. Meanwhile slice potatoes thinly.

Remove baking dish from oven and reduce temperature to 375 degrees F. Arrange ham in a single layer on top of onions. Arrange potatoes in one layer over ham. Pour in the eggs and sprinkle cheese evenly over the top. Season with pepper. (The country ham is quite salty, so the frittata should need no added salt.)

Return baking dish to oven and bake for 25 to 30 minutes, or until eggs are set and the frittata is puffed and lightly browned on top. Serve hot, warm, or cold.

— 6 SERVINGS —

Plum Preserve Butter

Fruited butters can be made with almost any well-flavored preserve, using the same proportions as below. If using marmalades omit the lemon juice.

¾ cup (1½ sticks) unsalted butter, softened
3 tablespoons plum preserves
1½ teaspoons lemon juice

In a food processor or small mixing bowl, combine butter, preserves, and lemon juice and process or beat until well blended. Transfer to a small crock or serving dish, cover, and refrigerate until well chilled.

Remove from the refrigerator about 1 hour before serving so that butter is spreadable.

— MAKES ABOUT 1 CUP —

Tropical Fruit Compote

If the pineapple is very ripe, this compote will need no sugar. The cook's reward is to eat the bits of sweet mango that cling to the pit.

1 medium-sized ripe pineapple, peeled and cored
1 ripe papaya, peeled, halved, and seeded
1 ripe mango, peeled and pitted
2 ripe bananas
¼ cup dry white wine
1 tablespoon dark rum
Sugar, if desired

To check the ripeness of a pineapple, pull one of the tiny leaves at the base of its foliage. If the leaf comes off, the fruit is ripe; if not, the pineapple is not yet ready to eat. Pineapples are most easily peeled with a cleaver. These are heavy and give the leverage needed to make peeling a quick, simple task.

Cut pineapple into 1-inch cubes. Slice papaya halves. Cut mango flesh into bite-size discs. Combine these fruits in a large bowl and toss gently. Cover and chill in refrigerator for up to 3 hours.

An hour before serving, remove fruit from refrigerator. Peel bananas and slice into fruit bowl. Sprinkle mixture with white wine and rum and toss. Taste for sweetness. If tart, sprinkle lightly with sugar and toss again.

Spoon into an attractive serving dish and serve.

— 6 SERVINGS (ABOUT 8 CUPS) —

COMMAND PERFORMANCE

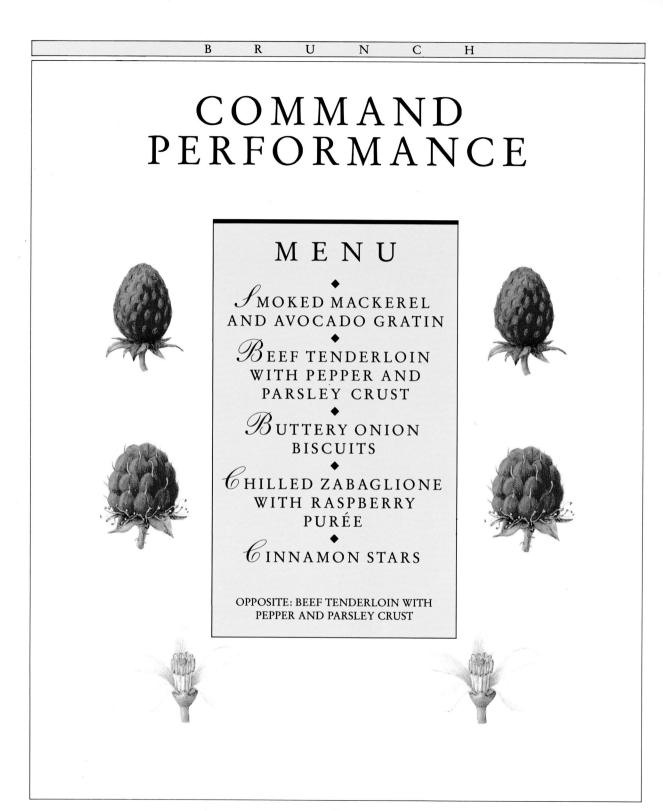

MENU

◆

*S*MOKED MACKEREL
AND AVOCADO GRATIN

◆

*B*EEF TENDERLOIN
WITH PEPPER AND
PARSLEY CRUST

◆

*B*UTTERY ONION
BISCUITS

◆

*C*HILLED ZABAGLIONE
WITH RASPBERRY
PURÉE

◆

*C*INNAMON STARS

OPPOSITE: BEEF TENDERLOIN WITH
PEPPER AND PARSLEY CRUST

Smoked Mackerel and Avocado Gratin

Although ramekins are
needed for two of the
recipes in this brunch
menu, the custards can
be unmolded well in ad-
vance of mealtime, free-
ing the ramekins for use
with the first course.

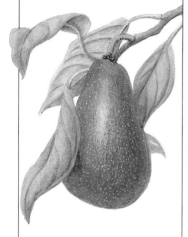

If smoked mackerel is
unavailable, substitute
fillet of smoked haddock
or of smoked cod. In
which case, place a 12- to
14-ounce piece of either
in a pan just large
enough to hold it com-
fortably and pour
enough boiling water
over the fish to cover it.
Cover with a lid or plate
and let steep for 5 to 10
minutes, depending on
the thickness of the fish;
then drain off the water.
Transfer the fish to paper
towels and pat it to ab-
sorb any excess water.

THE SAUCE FOR THIS DISH CAN BE MADE UP TO A DAY IN ADVANCE,
then brought back to a simmer before assembling, and the fish can be
skinned and broken into pieces ahead. But the mackerel and all other
ingredients should not be combined until just before the ramekins are to
be put under the broiler.

5	tablespoons unsalted butter
4	tablespoons flour
2½	cups milk
12	ounces boneless smoked mackerel
2	cups diced avocado (1 large or 2 small)
	Salt
	Freshly ground pepper
5	tablespoons grated Parmesan cheese

In a heavy, medium-sized saucepan, melt 4 tablespoons of the butter
over low heat. Add flour and stir until smooth. Simmer for 2 minutes,
stirring. Pour in the milk and stir over medium-high heat for 4 to 6
minutes, or until the sauce comes to a boil and thickens to the consistency of light cream. Simmer gently, uncovered, for 20 minutes, stirring
occasionally.

Lift the skin from the mackerel fillets, scrape away any soft fat that
adheres to the flesh, and break the fish into rough half-bite-size chunks;
there should be about 2 cups.

Preheat the broiler.

Remove sauce from the heat, stir in mackerel and avocado, and
season lightly with salt and pepper. Return saucepan to the heat and
warm the mixture for 1 to 2 minutes, or until avocado and fish are heated
through. Divide mixture among 8 individual ramekins. Sprinkle about 2
teaspoons of the Parmesan cheese over the top of each ramekin and set
them on a broiler pan.

Place under the broiler for 1 to 2 minutes, or until cheese is melted
and sauce is just starting to bubble around the edges. Serve immediately.

— 8 SERVINGS —

ℬEEF TENDERLOIN WITH PEPPER AND PARSLEY CRUST

THE TENDERLOIN CAN BE EATEN ALONE OR SANDWICHED BETWEEN split and buttered biscuits to make miniature tenderloin sandwiches.

2 pounds beef tenderloin, trimmed
2 teaspoons whole black peppercorns
2 teaspoons whole white peppercorns
2 teaspoons whole green peppercorns
2 teaspoons coarse salt
4 tablespoons butter, very soft
1 cup loosely packed flat-leaf parsley, chopped

TO SERVE
1 large bunch flat-leaf parsley

Allow tenderloin to come to room temperature before cooking.

Preheat oven to 450 degrees F.

Wrap black, white, and green peppercorns in a dish cloth or a double thickness of cheesecloth and crack with a wooden mallet or the bottom of a heavy skillet. Set aside on a large plate along with the salt. In a small bowl, combine butter and chopped parsley, beat until smooth, and rub mixture generously over tenderloin. Roll tenderloin in the crushed peppercorn mixture, coating all sides completely.

Roast tenderloin on a rack in a shallow baking pan in the center of hot oven for 25 to 30 minutes, or until a meat thermometer inserted into the center registers 130 degrees F., basting meat every 10 minutes as it cooks. (Meat will be rare.) Remove from the oven and let cool to room temperature, about 1 hour.

Using a very sharp knife, slice meat thinly and arrange overlapping slices in the center of a large serving platter. Surround meat generously with parsley. Serve at room temperature.

— 8 SERVINGS —

For a different presentation, offer a choice of British condiments with the beef: for example, a robust mustard and a piquant, creamy horse-radish sauce.

ℬUTTERY ONION BISCUITS

THESE VERY LIGHT BISCUITS ARE QUICKLY MADE, AND BECAUSE THE dough is cut into squares the re-shaping of scraps that comes with using a round cutter is avoided. Brushing the tops with buttermilk gives them a shine; using melted butter instead leaves the tops just as nicely browned but not shiny.

2   cups flour
3   teaspoons baking powder
½   teaspoon baking soda
½   teaspoon salt
½   cup (1 stick) plus 3 tablespoons butter
2   green onions, thinly sliced
¾   cup plus 2 tablespoons buttermilk

Preheat oven to 425 degrees F.

Sift flour, baking powder, baking soda, and salt into a large mixing bowl.

In a small skillet, melt 1 tablespoon of the butter over medium-low heat, add green onions, and sauté until softened but not browned, about 3 minutes. Remove from heat and let cool.

Cut remaining butter into small pieces and add to dry ingredients. Using knives or a pastry cutter, cut butter into flour mixture until mixture resembles coarse crumbs. Make a well in the center of mixture, add green onions and ¾ cup of the buttermilk, and mix just until a sticky dough forms. Turn dough out onto a lightly floured surface and knead 15 to 20 times. Roll or pat dough into a ½-inch-thick square. Using a sharp knife, cut into sixteen 2-inch squares. Place biscuits 2 inches apart on a baking sheet, brush tops with remaining buttermilk, and bake in the center of hot oven for 12 to 15 minutes, or until they are well risen and lightly browned on top.

Serve warm with butter.

— MAKES 16 BISCUITS —

CINNAMON STARS

THESE VERY CRISP, LIGHTLY SPICED COOKIES MAKE A LOVELY CHRIST-
mas treat.

1   cup flour
1½ teaspoons ground cinnamon
    Pinch salt
½ cup (1 stick) unsalted butter, softened
½ cup firmly packed light brown sugar
1   large egg yolk
2   tablespoons granulated sugar

Cinnamon Quill.

Sift flour, cinnamon, and salt together onto a sheet of waxed paper.

In a large mixing bowl, cream butter and brown sugar together until light and fluffy. Add egg yolk and beat until light. Add flour mixture and blend well. Cover and chill cookie dough in refrigerator for at least 1 hour or overnight.

Preheat oven to 350 degrees F.

Divide dough in half. On a lightly floured surface, roll out half of dough ⅛ inch thick. Using a 2½-inch star-shaped cookie cutter, cut out cookies and place them 2 inches apart on a lightly greased baking sheet. Roll and cut out second half of dough and arrange on baking sheet. Sprinkle cookies with granulated sugar.

Bake in the center of hot oven for 7 to 8 minutes, or until firm and just beginning to brown around the edges. Transfer to a wire rack and let cool. Store in a tightly covered container.

— MAKES ABOUT 30 COOKIES —

To turn these star-shaped cookies into edible decorations for the Christmas tree, carefully work a small hole into one of the points of the baked but still warm cookies, using a sharp metal skewer. When the cookies are cool thread a red ribbon through the hole and hang the Cinnamon Star on the tree.

Cinnamomum zeylanicum

CHILLED ZABAGLIONE WITH RASPBERRY PURÉE

SMOOTHER THAN A BAKED CUSTARD, BUT LIGHTER THAN A BAVARIAN, this molded dessert can be served with any fruit purée. When serving it as a dinner dessert, offer whipped cream as an accompaniment as well as the purée.

2 cups milk
1 package unflavored gelatin
1 tablespoon cornstarch
⅓ cup sugar
6 large egg yolks
¾ cup Marsala wine

PURÉE
1½ to 3 cups fresh raspberries
Sugar

This combination of flavors, turned around, produces another luscious dessert: fresh raspberries with warm zabaglione as a sauce. To serve 4, divide 3 cups raspberries among 4 individual dishes. In a medium mixing bowl whisk 4 egg yolks with 2 tablespoons sugar and ¾ cup Marsala. Just before serving, set the bowl into a saucepan of simmering water and whisk the mixture for about 5 minutes, or until it is light and fluffy. Spoon the zabaglione over the raspberries immediately (so that it does not continue cooking in the warm bowl) and serve.

Pour the milk into a small heavy saucepan, bring just to a boil, and remove immediately from the heat. Place ¼ cup cold water in a small bowl and sprinkle with the gelatin.

In a medium bowl, combine cornstarch and sugar, then whisk in the egg yolks until the mixture is smooth. Slowly pour half the hot milk into the egg mixture, whisking constantly. Pour the egg-milk mixture slowly back into the milk remaining in the saucepan and stir over medium heat until the custard thickens and begins to bubble. Stir softened gelatin into the custard until dissolved. Pour the custard into a mixing bowl and let cool for 5 minutes. Stir in the Marsala. Divide mixture among 8 individual ramekins or pour it into a single 1-quart bowl or mold. Chill in the refrigerator until set, about 1½ hours for ramekins or 2½ hours for a 1-quart mold.

Purée raspberries in a blender or food processor. Pass purée through a sieve, add sugar to taste, and stir until sugar dissolves.

To serve, run a knife carefully around the inside edges of the ramekins and gently turn the custards onto individual dessert plates or a single serving dish. Spoon a little of the raspberry purée around or over the custards decoratively and serve remaining purée separately in a bowl or pitcher.

— 8 SERVINGS —

LUNCH

LUNCH IN THE OLD DAIRY

MENU

◆

*B*UTTERMILK SQUASH SOUP

◆

*B*READ SALAD

◆

*W*ALNUT BISCUITS WITH STILTON

◆

*F*RESH PEARS

OPPOSITE: BUTTERMILK SQUASH SOUP, WALNUT BISCUITS, STILTON, FRESH PEARS, AND BREAD SALAD

*B*READ SALAD

A COLORFUL ASSORTMENT OF DICED VEGETABLES TOSSED WITH BREAD cubes to absorb their juices makes a handsome, light main course for lunch. The salad can be made a day before, to the point where the bread is added, and refrigerated, but bring the ingredients to room temperature before serving.

For a hotter, more fragrant dressing, 2 to 3 tablespoons Crabtree & Evelyn Olive and Sunflower Oil with Herbs may be used instead of the same amount of olive oil.

3 to 4 ripe plum tomatoes (about ½ pound)
1 loaf day-old French or Italian bread (about ½ pound), thickly sliced

DRESSING
6 tablespoons olive oil
2 tablespoons sunflower oil
4 tablespoons red-wine vinegar
1 tablespoon minced fresh basil leaves
   Salt
   Freshly ground black pepper

1 small cucumber, seeded and diced (about ⅔ cup)
1 small red onion, diced (about ¼ cup)
1 small sweet yellow pepper, cored, seeded, and diced (about ⅓ cup)
1 tablespoon drained capers
1 small head radicchio, shredded (about 1 cup, loosely packed)
¼ head romaine, shredded (about 1 cup, loosely packed)

TO SERVE
10 radicchio leaves
10 romaine leaves
3 fresh basil leaves

Into a medium saucepan of boiling water plunge the tomatoes (one at a time) and boil over high heat for 30 seconds. Drain, rinse in cold water, and peel. Cut each tomato in half and gently scoop out and discard seeds. Dice tomatoes and place in a large mixing bowl.

Tear bread slices into rough ½-inch pieces and add to the mixing bowl.

In another bowl, whisk together olive oil, sunflower oil, vinegar, and basil. Season with salt and pepper. Add cucumber, onion, sweet pepper, and capers to the vinaigrette and toss. Let stand for 20 to 30 minutes.

Add vegetable-vinaigrette mixture to bread and tomatoes and toss to mix well. Let stand for 30 minutes to 1 hour to allow bread to absorb juices.

Just before serving, add shredded radicchio and romaine and toss. To serve, line an attractive salad bowl or serving platter with the whole radicchio and romaine leaves. Spoon bread salad onto the bed of leaves and garnish with basil leaves.

— 4 GENEROUS SERVINGS —

BUTTERMILK SQUASH SOUP

THIS SOUP CAN BE MADE AHEAD AND GENTLY REHEATED, BUT DO NOT let it boil. For a summer version, use nine 4- to 5-inch zucchini in place of the butternut squash. Dice them and cook with the other vegetables in light oil instead of butter. Substitute 2 teaspoons minced fresh dill for the rosemary and serve hot or chilled.

3 tablespoons butter
1 medium butternut squash (about 1½ pounds), peeled, seeded, and cut into cubes
1 medium onion, coarsely chopped
1 medium carrot, coarsely chopped
1 rib celery, coarsely chopped
2 cups chicken stock
1 teaspoon minced fresh rosemary leaves, or ¼ teaspoon dried
1 cup buttermilk
Salt
Freshly ground pepper

TO SERVE
Sprigs of fresh rosemary

Melt butter in a large heavy saucepan. Add squash, onion, carrot, and celery, cover partially, and gently cook vegetables over medium-low heat for 10 minutes, or until softened. Add stock and rosemary. Cover and simmer over medium heat for about 15 minutes, or until vegetables are very soft. Remove pan from heat and let mixture cool slightly.

Purée mixture in a food processor or a food mill. Pour into a clean saucepan, gradually stir in buttermilk, and season with salt and pepper. Cover and cook gently until heated through.

Ladle into shallow soup bowls and garnish each with fresh rosemary.

— 4 SERVINGS (ABOUT 5 CUPS) —

Adding the buttermilk slowly to the hot soup base, stirring all the while, prevents curdling.

Walnut Biscuits

THIS BISCUIT DOUGH CAN BE MIXED, PATTED OUT, AND CUT IN ADvance, then frozen on baking sheets. Allow to defrost before baking.

1 cup all-purpose flour
1 cup finely ground walnuts
¼ cup salted butter, cut into pieces and softened

Preheat oven to 400 degrees F.

Combine flour and walnuts in a food processor or large mixing bowl and process or stir to blend. Add butter and process 10 to 15 seconds or blend briefly by hand until a soft dough forms.

On a well-floured surface, pat dough out ¼ inch thick. Using a lightly floured 2-inch cookie cutter, cut out dough, and place rounds on a lightly buttered baking sheet. Bake in the center of oven for 15 minutes, or until biscuits are nicely browned on the bottom. Let cool slightly in the pan. Serve with Stilton and fresh pears.

— MAKES 16 BISCUITS —

These biscuits are delicious eaten with Stilton (still the king of English cheeses) as well as with fresh pears. Stilton is at its best in the autumn and early winter.

In cooking, stir crumbled Stilton into a celery soup just before serving or melt it over hamburgers and steak during the last few moments under the broiler.

71

CHOWDER LUNCH

M E N U

◆

*C*RAB AND SWEET CORN
CHOWDER

◆

*B*ROCCOLI IN LEMON
VINAIGRETTE

◆

*B*ROWN SODA BREAD

◆

*P*OTTED CHEDDAR
CHEESE

◆

*R*ED FRUIT SORBET

OPPOSITE: BROCCOLI IN LEMON
VINAIGRETTE, BROWN SODA BREAD, AND
CRAB AND SWEET CORN CHOWDER

Broccoli in Lemon Vinaigrette

THIS SALAD GOES PARTICULARLY WELL WITH BROILED MEATS.

Lemon is an agreeable seasoning for hot broccoli as well. Add the fresh lemon juice to hot clarified butter according to taste and spike it with a touch of Tabasco, if desired. Pour it into a small warmed pitcher or sauce boat and pass separately.

1   large bunch fresh broccoli (about 2 pounds), trimmed and cut into 4-inch stalks

LEMON VINAIGRETTE
1   tablespoon fresh lemon juice
2   tablespoons white-wine vinegar
1   teaspoon Dijon-style mustard
½   cup vegetable oil
¼   teaspoon freshly grated lemon zest
½   teaspoon salt
    Pinch freshly ground black pepper
    Tabasco, or other hot pepper sauce, if desired

TO SERVE
½   red onion, thinly sliced (about ¼ cup)
8   thin slices lemon

In a large saucepan of lightly salted boiling water cook broccoli until crisp-tender, about 3 minutes. Drain and refresh broccoli under cold water. Shake off excess water and drain on paper towels. Place on a serving dish, cover tightly with plastic wrap, and chill.

In a small bowl, whisk together lemon juice, vinegar, and mustard. Whisk in oil. Add lemon zest, salt, and pepper and season with Tabasco, if desired.

Just before serving, toss the broccoli with the vinaigrette and arrange on a platter with the red onion slices. Garnish with lemon slices.

— 4 TO 6 SERVINGS —

Lemon Bonbons

CRAB AND SWEET CORN CHOWDER

LIKE MOST CHOWDERS, THIS DEVELOPS A DEEPER FLAVOR IF ALLOWED to stand for a few hours or overnight before serving. In this case, make sure that it cools uncovered; otherwise the broth may sour. Reheat the chowder gently before serving.

- 3 ounces bacon, finely diced (½ cup)
- 1 medium onion, chopped
- 1 bay leaf
- ½ teaspoon dried thyme
- 2 medium potatoes, peeled and diced (about 2 cups)
- 2 cups fresh corn kernels or thawed frozen corn kernels
- 1 cup half-and-half
- 1 cup milk
- ½ pound cooked, cleaned crab meat or lobster meat
- 2 tablespoons dry sherry
  Salt
  Freshly ground pepper

  TO SERVE
- 1 tablespoon chopped parsley

In a large heavy saucepan, cook bacon over low heat until fat is rendered and meat is crisp, about 15 minutes. Transfer bacon with a slotted spoon to paper towels to drain and reserve for garnish.

Add onion to fat remaining in saucepan and cook over medium heat until softened and translucent but not browned, about 5 minutes. Break bay leaf in half and add to pan. Add thyme, potatoes, and 1½ cups water. Bring to a simmer over medium heat, then cover, reduce heat to low, and simmer for 20 minutes.

Stir in corn, half-and-half, and milk. Bring back to a simmer and cook, uncovered, for 5 minutes. Add crab meat and simmer 2 to 3 minutes longer, or until potatoes are tender. Stir in sherry. Season with salt and pepper.

Ladle into individual serving bowls, garnish each with chopped parsley and the crisp bacon, and serve hot.

— 4 TO 6 SERVINGS (ABOUT 1½ QUARTS) —

Chowder, a classic of American cooking, is a gift from France. In times past, Breton fishermen made a communal stew from their catch, cooking it in an iron pot, a chaudière, *which gave its name to the dish. The pot and its contents traveled with the fishermen to Newfoundland and then through the eastern reaches of Canada to New England.*

BROWN SODA BREAD

THIS MAKES A FINE TEA BREAD, PARTICULARLY IF ¾ CUP RAISINS OR currants are stirred into the dough after it has been kneaded.

2 cups all-purpose flour
1¾ cups whole-wheat flour
1 teaspoon baking soda
1 teaspoon baking powder
1 teaspoon salt
4 tablespoons unsalted butter, cut into pieces
2 cups buttermilk (see Note)

Preheat oven to 375 degrees F.

Combine all-purpose and whole-wheat flours, baking soda, baking powder, and salt in a food processor and pulse with on/off motion to mix. Add butter and process for 15 seconds. With motor running, pour in buttermilk through feed tube and process for 10 seconds, or until a wet but manageable dough forms.

Turn dough out onto a well-floured board and shape lightly into an 8-inch round. Cut a deep cross in the center of the loaf. Bake on a buttered cookie sheet in the center of the oven for 1 hour, or until the loaf sounds hollow when thumped lightly on the bottom. Turn out onto a wire rack and let cool.

Serve warm in thick slices or cold and thinly sliced.

— MAKES 10 TO 12 THICK SLICES —

Note: If buttermilk is not available, in a bowl combine 2 tablespoons vinegar with 2 cups milk.

POTTED CHEDDAR CHEESE

THIS IS A SIMPLE POTTED CHEESE, OF WHICH VARIATIONS ABOUND. White wine may be substituted for Madeira, and the mixture can be flavored with a generous pinch of cayenne, ¼ teaspoon grated nutmeg or ground mace, 2 to 3 teaspoons of prepared mustard, or ½ to 1 teaspoon curry powder. For an herb cheese, add 2 tablespoons finely chopped fresh thyme, chives, sage, or savory, or 2 teaspoons dried.

Potting is a traditional English method of preserving—for the short term—meat, fish, and cheese. With cheese, pieces too dry or small for the cheese board are transformed into a mellow dish that is also thought to be more digestible than cheese as is. Butter, seasonings, and cream or wine are the other basic ingredients. The result tastes of fine cooking, not frugality.

Cheddar or any mild cheese is the obvious candidate for potting, but a blue cheese mixed with butter and brandy is delicious too. Or blend blue and Cheddar cheeses together.

½ pound sharp Cheddar cheese, grated
6 tablespoons unsalted butter
2 tablespoons Madeira or medium-dry sherry

In a food processor, blend the cheese and butter until mixture forms a ball. Add Madeira and process until the mixture is well blended and softened.

Transfer mixture to a small bowl and serve at room temperature surrounded by bread or crackers.

— 4 TO 6 SERVINGS —

ℛED FRUIT SORBET

IF FRESH STRAWBERRIES ARE NOT AVAILABLE, SUBSTITUTE TWO 10-ounce packages frozen ones in light syrup, omitting the sugar and sugar syrup.

1 pint fresh strawberries (about 2 cups), hulled
4 cups red seedless grapes
1 cup sugar
2 tablespoons Cognac or brandy

Purée berries and grapes in a food processor.

In a medium saucepan, combine sugar with 2 cups water and bring to a boil, swirling pan from time to time, until sugar is dissolved. Cook over medium heat for 1 minute. Stir puréed fruit into sugar syrup and cook at a gentle simmer over low heat for 5 minutes.

Strain mixture through a medium-mesh sieve set over a large bowl, pressing firmly with the back of a wooden spoon to extract as much juice and pulp as possible. Discard contents of sieve. Stir Cognac into sorbet base and chill in refrigerator for at least 30 minutes.

Pour mixture into container of an ice cream or sorbet machine and prepare according to manufacturer's instructions. Pack into a container and freeze for at least 3 hours.

— MAKES 1 QUART —

SOUP AND SANDWICH LUNCH

M E N U

◆

*L*EEK AND KALE SOUP

◆

*C*HICKEN PAILLARD
SANDWICHES WITH
WATERCRESS AND
MUSHROOMS

◆

*R*ASPBERRIES WITH
PEACH PURÉE

◆

*C*HOCOLATE WAFERS

OPPOSITE: CHICKEN PAILLARD
SANDWICHES WITH WATERCRESS AND
MUSHROOMS

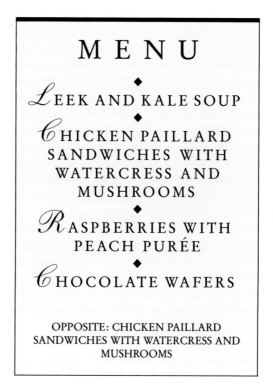

LEEK AND KALE SOUP

A VARIATION OF THE TRADITIONAL FRENCH POTATO AND LEEK SOUP, this delicately flavored mixture calls for a well-seasoned stock. It is also delicious cold, in which case a light vegetable oil should be substituted for the butter.

3   tablespoons butter
1   medium onion, chopped
2   shallots, chopped (optional)
4   cups thinly sliced leeks (white and light green parts only)
1   clove garlic
1½ cups peeled, coarsely chopped potatoes
5   to 6 cups chicken stock
    Bouquet garni, composed of 1 sprig parsley, 1 bay leaf, and 1 sprig each (or ¼ teaspoon dried each) marjoram, thyme, and rosemary, tied together in a cheesecloth bag
2   cups de-ribbed, finely shredded kale
1   tablespoon fresh minced marjoram leaves, or 1 teaspoon dried marjoram
½ cup heavy cream
1   to 2 teaspoons fresh lemon juice
    Salt
    Freshly ground pepper

TO SERVE
¼ cup minced fresh chives or green onions

In a large heavy saucepan, melt the butter, add onion, shallots, and leeks, and simmer, covered, over very low heat for 10 minutes, stirring occasionally to prevent vegetables from browning. Add garlic, potatoes, 4 cups of the stock, and bouquet garni. Cover partially and simmer over medium-low heat for 15 to 20 minutes, or until potatoes are tender.

Discard bouquet garni. Let soup cool slightly, then purée in a food processor or blender and return the mixture to the saucepan.

Add kale and marjoram and simmer over medium-low heat for 15 minutes. Stir in cream and simmer 5 minutes longer. Add enough of the remaining stock to dilute mixture to desired consistency. Season to taste with lemon juice, salt, and pepper.

Serve hot, sprinkled with chives or green onions.

— 6 SERVINGS —

CHOCOLATE WAFERS

AS WITH OTHER ICE-BOX COOKIES, THESE CAN BE FROZEN AS AN uncooked log of dough and thawed just before baking.

1   cup all-purpose flour
½   teaspoon baking powder
¼   teaspoon baking soda
     Pinch salt
     Pinch freshly ground pepper
6   tablespoons unsalted butter, softened
¼   cup firmly packed light brown sugar
¼   cup granulated sugar
1   large egg yolk
1   teaspoon vanilla extract
1   ounce unsweetened chocolate, melted (see Note)

Sift flour, baking powder, baking soda, salt, and pepper onto a sheet of waxed paper.

In a large mixing bowl or food processor, cream together butter, brown sugar, and granulated sugar until mixture is light and fluffy. Add egg yolk and beat until mixture is very well blended. Beat in vanilla and chocolate. Add dry ingredients and mix by hand or with an electric mixer at low speed until well blended.

Form dough into a smooth log about 1½ inches in diameter. Wrap in waxed paper and chill for at least 3 hours or up to 2 days.

Preheat oven to 375 degrees F.

Using a sharp knife, slice dough ⅛ inch thick. Place wafers 1½ inches apart on ungreased baking sheets and bake in the center of oven for 7 to 9 minutes, or until gentle pressure of a fingertip leaves no mark on the surface. Transfer wafers to wire racks and let cool completely. Store tightly covered.

— MAKES ABOUT 3 DOZEN COOKIES —

Note: To melt chocolate, soften it in a small saucepan set over a larger saucepan of simmering water.

CHICKEN PAILLARD SANDWICHES WITH WATERCRESS AND MUSHROOMS

If fresh wild mushrooms are unavailable, use dried ones instead, allowing 1½ ounces dried for 8 ounces fresh.

Rinse the dried mushrooms quickly under cold water to remove any dirt, place them in a small bowl, and pour warm water over them to cover. Let them soak for 30 minutes, or until plumped, then drain them through a fine-meshed sieve set over another small bowl. Gently squeeze excess liquid from the mushrooms before adding them to the dish.

A FLAMBOYANT-LOOKING BUT LIGHT MAIN-COURSE SANDWICH, THIS can also be made with 3 cups trimmed, thinly sliced domestic mushrooms.

1 pound boneless chicken breasts, skinned, split, and cut into 8 thin escallops	2 or 3 sprigs fresh tarragon, or ¼ teaspoon dried tarragon leaves
Salt	1 bunch watercress, washed, drained, and tough stems removed
Freshly ground pepper	
1½ tablespoons unsalted butter	⅓ cup mayonnaise
1½ tablespoons olive oil	4 Kaiser or large French rolls
8 ounces fresh edible wild mushrooms	
1 tablespoon minced shallots	TO SERVE
1 tablespoon tarragon vinegar	Several sprigs fresh watercress
2 tablespoons chicken stock or white wine	

Season chicken on both sides with salt and pepper.

In a large skillet, melt 1 tablespoon of the butter with 1 tablespoon of the oil over medium-high heat. Add chicken and sauté, in batches if necessary, for 30 to 60 seconds per side, or until lightly browned and cooked through. Remove and keep warm. Do not rinse skillet.

In skillet, melt remaining ½ tablespoon butter with remaining ½ tablespoon oil, add mushrooms and shallots, and cook over medium-low heat for about 2 minutes, or until shallots are softened. Season lightly with salt and pepper. Remove mushroom mixture with a slotted spoon and set aside, covered to keep it warm.

Preheat broiler.

Add vinegar and stock to the skillet and deglaze over medium-high heat, scraping up any browned bits. Stir in tarragon and simmer mixture for 10 to 15 seconds. Add watercress and toss over low heat for 5 seconds, just until leaves are coated. Remove watercress with a slotted spoon and set aside. Remove the skillet from the heat and stir in the mayonnaise.

Cut rolls in half and place under hot broiler until lightly toasted.

To assemble, spread roll halves with the flavored mayonnaise. Arrange 2 chicken paillards on the bottom half of each roll. Top chicken with mushrooms and watercress. Cover with tops of rolls, or serve open-face style.

Place sandwiches on individual plates, garnish each with watercress sprigs, and serve.

— 4 SERVINGS —

ℛASPBERRIES WITH PEACH PUREE

THIS IS A LIGHTER COMBINATION OF THE FLAVORS IN ESCOFFIER'S famous Peach Melba, created for Dame Nellie Melba in 1894. The following recipe is equally delicious served in meringue shells for a more formal meal or arranged around a square of English Gingerbread (page 126) to round off an informal supper. The Cardamom Custard Sauce (page 242) or ½ to ¾ cup heavy cream, whipped, may be substituted for the *crème fraîche*.

The purée can be made several hours ahead but should be stirred before spooning on the plates. The raspberry vinegar holds the color of the peaches, adds a subtle tang, and heightens the flavor of the raspberries. Pears may be substituted for the peaches and can simply be peeled without being dipped first in boiling water.

4   medium peaches, peeled and the pits removed
2   to 3 teaspoons raspberry vinegar
2   tablespoons powdered sugar, or to taste
2   cups fresh raspberries
½   to ¾ cup *crème fraîche*

Purée the peaches in a food processor or a food mill fitted with the finest disk. (There should be about 1 cup purée.) Add the raspberry vinegar and enough of the powdered sugar to balance the taste. Refrigerate until serving time.

Divide the purée among 4 dessert plates, spooning it into a semicircle. Nestle a quarter of the raspberries beside each serving of purée and pass the *crème fraîche* separately.

— SERVES 4 —

To peel peaches, bring a medium saucepan of water to a boil. Drop 1 peach at a time gently into the boiling water, leave it for 5 seconds, and retrieve it by piercing the flesh with a fork. With a paring knife, slit the skin, which will then slip off easily.

CELEBRATING MAY

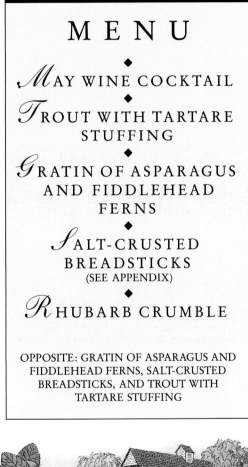

MENU

◆

*M*AY WINE COCKTAIL

◆

*T*ROUT WITH TARTARE
STUFFING

◆

*G*RATIN OF ASPARAGUS
AND FIDDLEHEAD
FERNS

◆

*S*ALT-CRUSTED
BREADSTICKS
(SEE APPENDIX)

◆

*R*HUBARB CRUMBLE

OPPOSITE: GRATIN OF ASPARAGUS AND
FIDDLEHEAD FERNS, SALT-CRUSTED
BREADSTICKS, AND TROUT WITH
TARTARE STUFFING

Sweet woodruff (Galium odoratum) is a shade-loving perennial with tiny white flowers. The delicate young leaves, when bruised, have the aroma of freshly cut hay. Woodruff is a classic flavoring for alcoholic drinks in Europe and can be easily grown in the garden.

MAY WINE COCKTAIL

THIS IS A VARIATION ON A TRADITIONAL GERMAN SPRINGTIME DRINK, *Maiwein* or *Maitrank*. At its simplest, it consists of Moselle or Rhine wine with sugar and sweet woodruff. Brandy, Benedictine, strawberries, oranges, and even Champagne grace more elaborate versions. If woodruff is unavailable, the combination of spicy white wine and raspberry syrup makes a delicious cocktail on its own.

8   sprigs tender, sweet woodruff, if available (see Note)
1   bottle medium-dry German white wine such as Riesling
    TO SERVE
8   teaspoons raspberry syrup or Framboise
    Sweet woodruff sprigs, if desired

Gently bruise woodruff leaves between the fingers and place in the bottle of wine. Recork and let steep in the refrigerator for 8 hours. Strain through a sieve, discarding woodruff leaves.

At serving time, place about 2 teaspoons of the raspberry syrup in the bottom of each of 4 stemmed hock or white-wine glasses. Fill almost to the rim with flavored wine and stir gently to combine. Float a small sprig of woodruff on surface of each cocktail, if desired.

— 4 SERVINGS —

Note: Use only tender young sprigs of woodruff; old leaves have too strong a flavor.

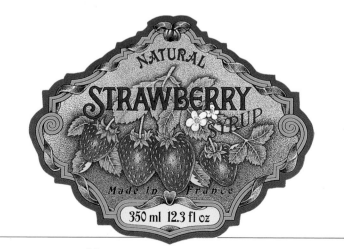

NATURAL
STRAWBERRY SYRUP
Made in France
350 ml 12.3 fl oz

TROUT WITH TARTARE STUFFING

A SIMPLE, WELL-FLAVORED STUFFING AND A STRIP OF BACON ADD TWO complementary tastes and textures to fresh trout. The fish can be stuffed early in the day and refrigerated until cooking time.

4   whole, pan-ready trout (10 to 12 ounces each)
    Salt
    Freshly ground pepper

    STUFFING
2   teaspoons butter
1   cup thinly sliced fresh mushrooms
1   cup bread crumbs
½   cup prepared tartare sauce
2   tablespoons finely minced fresh parsley
4   long slices bacon

    TO SERVE
    Parsley sprigs

Wipe trout cavities clean with paper towels and sprinkle lightly with salt and pepper.

To make the stuffing, melt the butter in a medium-sized skillet over high heat. Add mushrooms and sauté for 2 minutes, stirring continually, until mushrooms wilt and soften. Remove mushrooms from the heat with a slotted spoon and stir in bread crumbs, tartare sauce, and minced parsley. Season with salt and pepper.

Preheat broiler or build a medium-hot charcoal fire.

Fill trout cavities with stuffing and secure closure with toothpicks. Lay each trout on a slice of bacon, perpendicular to it, wrap ends of bacon around the middle, and tie once.

Place trout on a rack in a broiler pan or in a barbecue fish holder and cook for about 5 minutes per side, or until the bacon is cooked and the trout flesh becomes opaque.

Arrange trout on a bed of parsley sprigs on a platter or serve on individual plates garnished with parsley sprigs.

— 4 SERVINGS —

With trout—and almost all fish—freshness is of the essence. Fresh trout glistens, with shiny eyes that are not sunken or dull, resilient flesh, and a fresh, clean smell.

$\mathscr{G}$RATIN OF ASPARAGUS AND FIDDLEHEAD FERNS

FIDDLEHEADS ARE AVAILABLE FRESH OR FROZEN IN MANY SPECIALTY foods shops. If fiddleheads are not available, double the quantity of asparagus.

¾ pound thin fresh asparagus
¾ pound tender fresh fiddlehead ferns
¾ cup heavy cream
1 small clove garlic
2 teaspoons minced shallots
Salt
Freshly ground pepper
4 tablespoons fresh bread crumbs
1 tablespoon cornmeal
1 tablespoon grated Parmesan cheese
2 teaspoons unsalted butter, cut into small pieces

*Fiddleheads, the coiled new shoots of the ostrich fern (*Matteuccia struthiopteris)*, are named for their resemblance to the scroll of a violin.*

Snap off and discard the tough ends of the asparagus. Cut tips off about 2½ inches from tip ends and slice remainder of spears into ½-inch pieces. Rinse fiddleheads well, gently rubbing off any brown skin.

Bring a large saucepan of lightly salted water to a boil, add asparagus tips and pieces, and boil for 2 minutes. Using a slotted spoon, remove asparagus and plunge it into a bowl of cold water to stop the cooking and to preserve the color. Drain well. Add fiddleheads to the same boiling water and boil for 4 minutes. Drain fiddleheads, plunge them into cold water, and drain thoroughly.

Place cream and garlic clove in a small saucepan and simmer over low heat until cream is slightly thickened, about 10 minutes.

Preheat oven to 400 degrees F.

Sprinkle shallots evenly over the bottom of a generously buttered 1½-quart shallow flame-proof baking dish. Scatter asparagus pieces evenly over shallots. Arrange a neat row of asparagus tips, all tips pointing in the same direction, at one end of the dish. Lay a row of fiddleheads, coils facing same direction, next to asparagus tips. Continue to arrange alternating rows of asparagus tips and fiddleheads until dish is filled. Season with salt and pepper.

Discard garlic clove from thickened cream and pour cream over asparagus and fiddleheads. Combine bread crumbs, cornmeal, and

Parmesan cheese and sprinkle mixture evenly over vegetables. Dot with butter. (Casserole can be prepared up to this point in advance and refrigerated for several hours before baking.)

Bake for 5 to 8 minutes (or 15 to 20 minutes if casserole has been refrigerated for several hours before baking), or until heated through. Brown top of casserole under broiler for 2 to 3 minutes. Serve hot.

— 4 SERVINGS —

ℛHUBARB CRUMBLE

THE TARTNESS OF YOUNG RHUBARB SET AGAINST THE BUTTERY, SWEET crumble topping makes this a wonderful fruit pudding. Serve it at room temperature with a pitcher of heavy cream or with a good vanilla ice cream. Do not refrigerate before serving as the topping will lose some of its crispness.

1½ pounds fresh rhubarb, sliced (about 5 cups)
½ cup light corn syrup

CRUMBLE TOPPING
1 cup all-purpose flour
⅓ cup sugar
½ cup (1 stick) unsalted butter, softened

Preheat oven to 350 degrees F.

In a 1½-quart baking dish, about 8 inches in diameter, arrange rhubarb in a fairly level layer. Pour corn syrup evenly over rhubarb.

To make the topping, combine flour, sugar, and butter in a bowl and work ingredients together with the fingertips until it resembles coarse bread crumbs. Sprinkle topping lightly over rhubarb.

Bake in the center of the oven for 1 hour, or until a knife inserted into the center of the fruit pierces the rhubarb easily.

— 4 TO 5 SERVINGS —

TEMPTING FÊTE

MENU

◆

*B*RAISED HAM GLAZED
WITH ORANGE
MARMALADE

◆

*V*EGETABLES
PROVENÇALE

◆

*C*RUNCHY FENNEL SLAW

◆

WHOLE-WHEAT AND
POTATO CLOVERLEAF
ROLLS
(SEE APPENDIX)

◆

*O*RANGE FLOWER LAYER
CAKE

OPPOSITE: BRAISED HAM GLAZED WITH
ORANGE MARMALADE

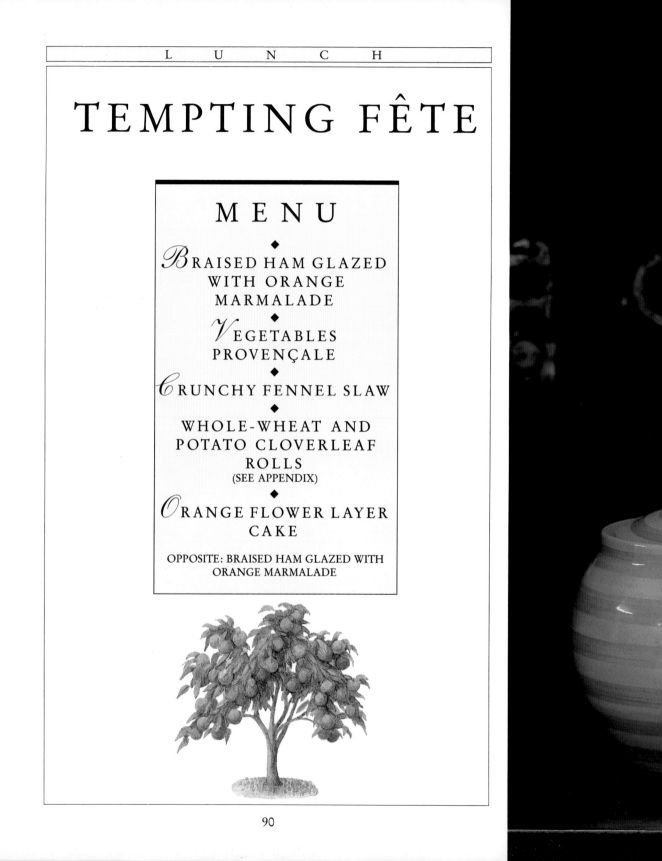

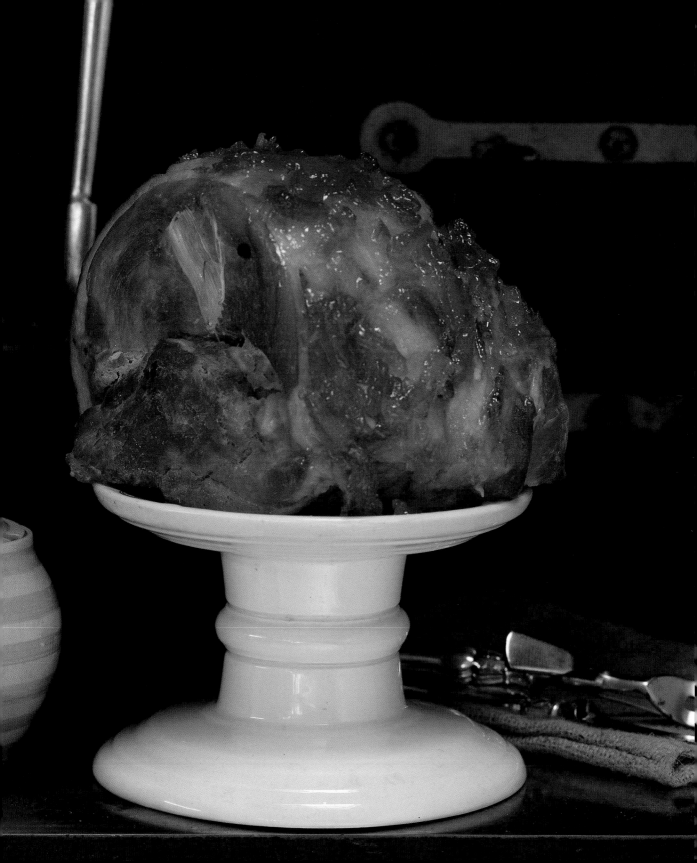

BRAISED HAM GLAZED WITH ORANGE MARMALADE

THIS MAKES A FINE AND PARTICULARLY MOIST CHANGE FROM THE more usual baked ham. Any orange marmalade makes a delicious glaze, and one flavored with ginger is even better. If the ham has a rind, carefully slice it from the meat, leaving a thin layer of fat, after braising but before glazing. Also before glazing cut a criss-cross diamond pattern into the remaining layer of fat.

If serving the ham hot, the cooking liquid makes an excellent sauce. Strain it into a saucepan, discarding the vegetables and seasonings. Taste the liquid to see if the flavor is sufficiently full; if not, boil it rapidly until the sauce becomes more concentrated.

This may be served as a thin sauce; if a slightly thicker consistency is preferred, for every cup of sauce whisk in a mixture of 1 teaspoon cornstarch and 1 tablespoon cold water. Bring the sauce to a boil, whisking constantly until it is thickened and the cloudiness of the cornstarch has cleared.

3 tablespoons light vegetable oil
2 carrots, finely chopped
2 ribs of celery, finely chopped
1 4- to 5-pound precooked, mildly cured ham
1 to 1½ cups chicken stock
1 to 1½ cups dry red wine
1 *bouquet garni* made with 1 bay leaf, 3 parsley sprigs, 2 thyme sprigs, and 1 strip orange rind, tied together with kitchen string in cheesecloth
8 to 10 black peppercorns
½ to ⅔ cup orange marmalade

Preheat the oven to 325° F.

In a deep heavy flame-proof casserole or baking dish large enough to hold the ham comfortably, heat the oil over high heat until it is hot but not smoking, add the carrot and celery, and cook the vegetables over medium heat, stirring occasionally, until soft but not browned.

Set the ham on the bed of vegetables and add the stock and wine in equal quantities until the liquid reaches halfway up the sides of the ham. Add the *bouquet garni* and the peppercorns and bring the liquid to a simmer. Cover the casserole with a lid or foil and bake the ham for 1 to 1¼ hours, basting 2 or 3 times with the braising liquid.

Remove the ham from the oven, transfer it to a roasting pan, and let it rest at room temperature. Raise the oven temperature to 450° F.

Spread about half the marmalade over the ham to make a thin layer of glaze and return the ham to the oven for 10 minutes. Spread the ham with another thin layer of marmalade and bake it for 10 minutes more. Let the ham cool and then chill it in the refrigerator before slicing.

— SERVES 8 TO 10 —

CRUNCHY FENNEL SLAW

7 cups finely shredded green cabbage (about ½ large
head), reserving large outer leaves for garnish
1 cup finely shredded fennel bulb
⅓ cup grated carrot
¼ cup thinly sliced red onion

FENNEL SEED DRESSING (SEE NOTE)
1 large egg yolk
4 teaspoons white-wine vinegar
½ teaspoon salt
¼ cup sunflower oil
¼ cup hazelnut oil
½ cup sour cream
½ teaspoon fennel seed
⅛ teaspoon freshly ground pepper
Pinch sugar

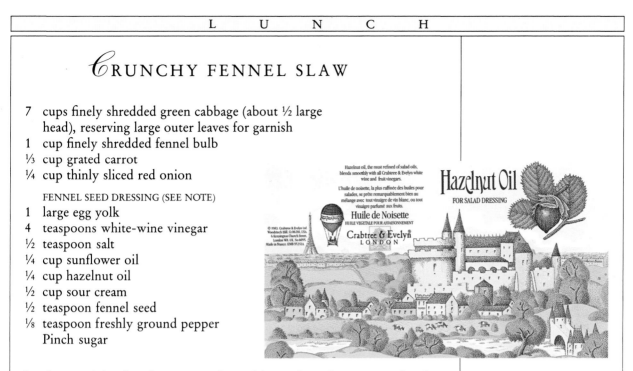

In a large mixing bowl, toss together cabbage, fennel, carrot, and onion.

To make dressing, in a food processor blend egg yolk, vinegar, and salt with an on-off motion or beat in a bowl with a wire whisk until blended. With processor running, slowly add a little of the oil through the feed tube until mixture starts to thicken. Add remaining oil in a thin, steady stream through feed tube until thoroughly incorporated. If mixing by hand, add oil a few drops at a time, beating constantly with a wire whisk, until mixture starts to thicken. Add remaining oil in a thin, steady stream, beating constantly, until well blended. Add sour cream, fennel seed, pepper, and sugar and process or whisk until blended.

Add dressing to shredded vegetables and toss until combined well. Cover and chill slaw for at least 30 minutes, but not more than 3 or 4 hours, before serving. (If dressing is added more than 4 hours ahead, slaw will become watery.)

To serve, line a salad bowl or large serving platter with reserved cabbage leaves and arrange slaw on top.

— 8 TO 10 SERVINGS —

Note: The dressing can be made in advance and stored in a covered container in the refrigerator until tossing with vegetables.

$\mathcal{V}$EGETABLES PROVENÇALE

AS ONLY A HINT OF GARLIC IS CALLED FOR, GARLIC LOVERS MAY WANT to add 1 to 3 minced garlic cloves to the onion in the last minute of frying. Once assembled, the casserole may be refrigerated for a day or may be frozen.

2 to 3 medium eggplants (about 2½ pounds), unpeeled and sliced into ½-inch rounds
 Salt
1 cup olive oil
6 zucchini (about 5 inches long each), sliced lengthwise into ½-inch strips
1 large sweet red pepper, seeds and membranes removed, flesh cut into ½-inch-wide strips
1 large sweet green pepper, seeds and membranes removed, flesh cut into ½-inch-wide strips
1 large onion, chopped
 Fresh ground black pepper
3 tablespoons chopped fresh basil, or 2 teaspoons dried
1 clove garlic, crushed
8 plum tomatoes, sliced
½ cup tomato juice
¾ cup fresh bread crumbs
¾ cup grated Monterey Jack cheese
¼ cup grated Parmesan cheese

Put the eggplant slices; sprinkled with salt, in a large colander and let them drain for 30 to 60 minutes.

Preheat the oven to 350 degrees F.

Spread 2 tablespoons of the oil on the bottom of each of 2 roasting pans. Wipe the salt and moisture from the eggplant slices and lay them, with the zucchini strips, in the pans. Sprinkle 1 tablespoon of the remaining oil over the vegetables, cover the pans with foil, and roast for an hour, turning the slices after 30 minutes.

Meanwhile, in a skillet cook the sweet peppers and onion in 4 to 6 tablespoons of the remaining oil with a sprinkling of salt and a few grinds of the black pepper over medium heat for about 5 minutes, or until softened. Stir in the basil.

Rub a 3-quart baking dish with the garlic clove and lightly oil it. Layer the 2 vegetable mixtures and the tomatoes in the dish. Pour the tomato juice over the vegetables and season, if necessary, with salt and pepper. Mix together the bread crumbs and cheeses and sprinkle over all. Finally, drizzle 1 tablespoon of the remaining oil over the top.

Bake the casserole, uncovered, for 1 hour, or until heated through, bubbling around the edges, and crusty on top.

— 8 TO 10 SERVINGS —

ORANGE FLOWER LAYER CAKE

THE CAKE LAYERS MAY BE MADE AHEAD AND FROZEN, THEN THAWED, assembled, and iced early on the day of serving. One cup of orange curd can be used to fill the cake in place of the marmalade mixture. Store leftover cake, tightly covered, in a cool place or in the refrigerator.

This cake celebrates the versatile orange. Orange rind, peel, flesh, juice, and blossoms contribute different tones of the orange flavor. And not just to sweet foods; dried bitter, or Seville, orange rind lends a special perfume to a bouquet garni, whereas the juice of a sweet, or blood, orange gives a lift to vinaigrettes for avocado and chicken salads.

CAKE
3 cups cake flour
4 teaspoons baking powder
½ teaspoon salt
1 cup unsalted butter, softened
2 cups sugar
4 large eggs, at room temperature
1½ tablespoons orange flower water
1 cup milk, at room temperature
  Grated zest of 1 orange

FILLING
1 cup orange marmalade, at room temperature
1 cup orange curd
1 teaspoon Grand Marnier or other orange-flavored liqueur or brandy

TO DECORATE
2 tablespoons powdered sugar
  Fresh orange flowers and leaves or thinly sliced orange zest

Preheat oven to 350 degrees F.

Sift flour, baking powder, and salt onto a sheet of waxed paper.

In a large mixing bowl, cream together butter and sugar until mixture is light and fluffy. Add eggs, one at a time, beating about 2 minutes after each addition. Beat in orange flower water.

Alternately add dry ingredients and milk to butter-egg mixture in 3 additions of dry ingredients and 2 of milk, mixing very gently, until batter is just blended. Stir in orange zest.

Butter three 9-inch round cake pans, line them with rounds of buttered parchment paper, and dust them with flour. Divide the batter among the pans and smooth tops.

Bake for 25 to 30 minutes, or until layers begin to pull away from sides of pans and a toothpick inserted in centers comes out clean. Let

For another version of this opulent dessert, make half the quantity of orange filling. Spread this on the bottom layer. Whip 1¼ cups heavy cream and fold in 1 grated square (1 ounce) of bitter chocolate; use this for the second filling. Set the third layer on the whipped cream and place a paper doily on top.

Refrigerate until an hour before serving. Just before bringing the cake to the table, sift 2 tablespoons powdered sugar over the doily and carefully lift off the doily, leaving a white lacy pattern on the top of the cake.

cool 10 minutes in pans. Carefully turn cakes out onto wire racks and let cool completely.

Meanwhile, in a small bowl, stir together marmalade, orange curd, and Grand Marnier and set aside.

To assemble cake, place one layer on a cake plate and on it spread half of filling evenly. Add second layer, spread evenly with remaining filling, and top with third layer. Sift the powdered sugar over the cake and garnish with orange flowers and leaves or with the orange zest.

— 12 SERVINGS —

PICNICS

WEATHER PERMITTING...

MENU

◆

*S*ALTED PINE NUTS

◆

*C*OOLING BORSCHT

◆

*C*HICKEN AND MELON
SALAD

◆

*L*IGHT HERBED RICE
CAKE

◆

*C*RESCENT MOONS

OPPOSITE: COOLING BORSCHT AND
SALTED PINE NUTS

Salted Pine Nuts

These tiny nuts, shaped like corn kernels, also give a distinctive texture and delicate nutty flavor to rice, vegetable dishes, and stuffings for meats, fish, and vegetables.

AFTER TOASTING PINE NUTS, LET THEM STAND FOR AN HOUR TO allow their flavor to develop. Or roast them a day before they are needed and store in an airtight container. They can also be sprinkled, in place of almonds, over chicken salad, trout, or lightly steamed snow peas turned quickly in butter.

1 cup pine nuts
2 teaspoons cold unsalted butter, diced
1 teaspoon finely ground sea salt

Preheat oven to 300 degrees F.

Spread pine nuts out in one layer on a baking sheet. Dot with butter. Roast in oven for 5 minutes. Stir nuts to coat evenly with melted butter. Continue roasting for 15 minutes, or until they are a deep golden, but not dark, brown. Remove from oven, sprinkle with salt, and let cool.

— MAKES 1 CUP —

Cooling Borscht

THIS BORSCHT, SERVED CHILLED HERE, MAY ALSO BE SERVED HOT, omitting the yogurt and topping each portion instead with a spoonful of sour cream just before serving.

1 pound raw beets (about 5 beets), peeled
1 onion, chopped
1 carrot, chopped
1 leek, washed and chopped
1 rib of celery, chopped
6 peppercorns
1 bay leaf
1 tablespoon red-wine or sherry vinegar
8 cups beef stock
1 tablespoon cornstarch
1 cup plain yogurt
2 to 4 tablespoons fresh lemon juice

For a hearty hot borscht, remove the bay leaf when the vegetables are softened and purée the soup. Add the grated beets, cook the soup until the beets are tender, and season with fresh lemon juice. Do not add the cornstarch.

Coarsely grate 2 beets and set aside. Slice remaining beets and combine in a large enamel or other non-reactive saucepan with onion, carrot, leek, celery, peppercorns, bay leaf, vinegar, and stock. Bring to a boil over high heat, reduce heat to low, and simmer, covered, for about 1 hour, or until the beets have faded to brownish pink and vegetables are very soft.

Strain liquid into another saucepan, pressing beets and vegetables with the back of a spoon to extract as much juice as possible. Discard beets and vegetables.

Add reserved grated beets to beet liquid, cover, and simmer over low heat for 15 minutes, or until tender.

In a small bowl, blend cornstarch with 1 tablespoon cold water. Stir into borscht and bring to a boil, stirring constantly. Remove from heat and let cool. Blend in yogurt and enough lemon juice to add a pleasant tartness. Cover and refrigerate until well chilled.

— 6 SERVINGS —

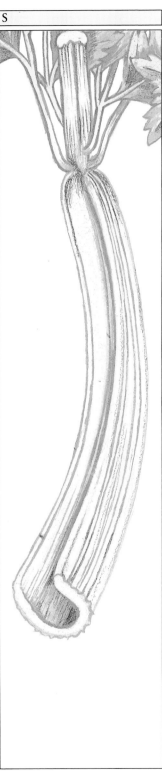

CHICKEN AND MELON SALAD

THE DARK MEAT OF CHICKEN THIGHS MARRIES WELL WITH THIS RICHLY flavored dressing. Meat from a 4-pound roast duck may also be used. The chicken (or duck) can be cooked the day before, and the dressing prepared well in advance.

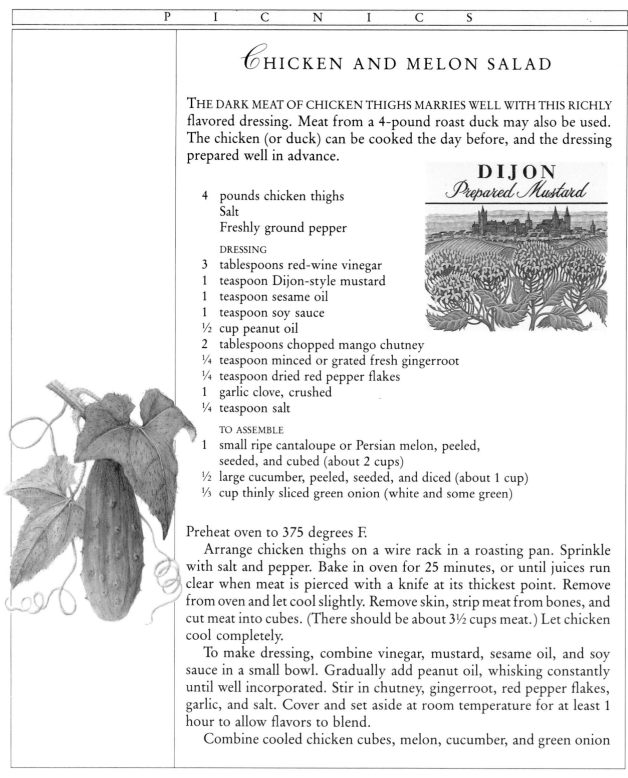

4   pounds chicken thighs
    Salt
    Freshly ground pepper

DRESSING
3   tablespoons red-wine vinegar
1   teaspoon Dijon-style mustard
1   teaspoon sesame oil
1   teaspoon soy sauce
½   cup peanut oil
2   tablespoons chopped mango chutney
¼   teaspoon minced or grated fresh gingerroot
¼   teaspoon dried red pepper flakes
1   garlic clove, crushed
¼   teaspoon salt

TO ASSEMBLE
1   small ripe cantaloupe or Persian melon, peeled,
    seeded, and cubed (about 2 cups)
½   large cucumber, peeled, seeded, and diced (about 1 cup)
⅓   cup thinly sliced green onion (white and some green)

Preheat oven to 375 degrees F.

Arrange chicken thighs on a wire rack in a roasting pan. Sprinkle with salt and pepper. Bake in oven for 25 minutes, or until juices run clear when meat is pierced with a knife at its thickest point. Remove from oven and let cool slightly. Remove skin, strip meat from bones, and cut meat into cubes. (There should be about 3½ cups meat.) Let chicken cool completely.

To make dressing, combine vinegar, mustard, sesame oil, and soy sauce in a small bowl. Gradually add peanut oil, whisking constantly until well incorporated. Stir in chutney, gingerroot, red pepper flakes, garlic, and salt. Cover and set aside at room temperature for at least 1 hour to allow flavors to blend.

Combine cooled chicken cubes, melon, cucumber, and green onion in a large bowl and toss. Cover bowl and refrigerate for up to 4 hours.

To assemble, remove garlic clove from dressing, whisk to blend, and pour enough over salad to thoroughly coat ingredients. Toss gently, taste for seasoning, and arrange on a serving platter.

— 6 SERVINGS —

$\mathcal{L}$IGHT HERBED RICE CAKE

FOR A PICNIC, SERVE THESE SQUARES OF CHEESE- AND HERB-FLAVORED rice warm or at room temperature. They are also delicious eaten hot with a tomato sauce and thin slices of cold rare roast lamb or beef.

1   cup uncooked medium-grain rice
1   teaspoon salt
4   tablespoons butter, melted
1   cup grated medium-sharp Cheddar cheese
2   tablespoons finely chopped onion
2   tablespoons minced fresh dill, or 2 teaspoons dried
¼   cup minced fresh parsley
1   large egg, lightly beaten
½   cup milk
¼   teaspoon Tabasco or other hot pepper sauce
    Pinch freshly ground black pepper

Preheat oven to 350 degrees F.

In a medium saucepan, combine rice, salt, and 2 cups water. Bring to a boil over high heat. Cover tightly, reduce heat to lowest setting, and cook for 15 to 18 minutes, or until rice is tender but still lightly firm to the bite. Remove from heat and fluff rice with a fork.

In a large mixing bowl, combine butter, cheese, onion, dill, parsley, egg, milk, Tabasco, and black pepper and blend well. Add rice and toss to combine well.

Press mixture evenly into a lightly buttered 8- or 9-inch-square baking dish. Bake in the center of oven for 35 to 40 minutes, or until rice is beginning to brown lightly around the edges and become crusty. Remove from oven and let cool for 20 minutes before cutting. Run a small knife around edges of dish and cut rice into 2-inch squares.

— 4 TO 6 SERVINGS —

CRESCENT MOONS

PASTRY DOUGH WITH A COMBINATION OF CREAM CHEESE AND BUTTER has a melting texture and delicate flavor. If an assortment of preserves is used, vary the slits on top of crescents or cut slits in the shape of small letters to indicate the flavor of the jam inside. If serving at home, dust turnovers lightly with powdered sugar just before serving.

1   cup all-purpose flour
½   teaspoon salt
3   ounces cold cream cheese, cut into small pieces
6   tablespoons cold unsalted butter, cut into small pieces
½ to ⅔ cup cherry preserves, or other thick fruit preserves
    or marmalade
1   large egg, beaten
2   teaspoons milk or cream

In a large mixing bowl, combine flour and salt. Add cream cheese and butter and blend with a fork or pastry cutter until mixture resembles coarse crumbs. Sprinkle with 2 tablespoons ice water and toss with a fork to moisten ingredients. If mixture seems dry, add 1 to 3 more teaspoons water, mixing until dough can be gathered into a ball. Flatten into a disk, wrap with plastic wrap or waxed paper, and chill for at least 30 minutes.

Preheat oven to 425 degrees F.

On a lightly floured surface, roll out dough to a thickness of ⅛ inch. Using a 4-inch biscuit or cookie cutter or a small plate as a guide, cut dough into circles. Re-roll scraps to make more circles. (There should be 12 to 15.)

Spoon 2 teaspoons of preserves into center of each pastry round. Brush edge of each with some of the beaten egg. Fold dough over preserves to form half moons. Press edges down firmly with your fingers, then press with the tines of a fork to seal well. Beat milk into the remaining beaten egg and brush mixture over the tops of the turnovers. Make a small slit in the top of each to allow steam to escape.

Arrange turnovers about an inch apart on an ungreased baking sheet. Bake in the center of oven for 18 to 20 minutes, or until the pastry is golden brown and crisp. Let turnovers cool on a wire rack.

— MAKES 12 TO 15 CRESCENTS —

Individual double-crust mincemeat tartlets are a traditional part of English Christmas feasting, eaten at teatime or at the end of a meal. Use this dough to make them particularly elegant. Shape them into crescent moons for a more generous proportion of mincemeat to pastry.

PUNTING DOWNSTREAM

MENU

◆

SHRIMP AND SCALLOP SALAD

◆

BASIL CORNBREAD AND BUTTER SANDWICHES

◆

CRUNCHY LEMON SYRUP CAKE

OPPOSITE: BASIL CORNBREAD AND
BUTTER SANDWICHES, CRUNCHY
LEMON SYRUP CAKE, AND SHRIMP
AND SCALLOP SALAD

ℐHRIMP AND SCALLOP SALAD

WHEN BAY SCALLOPS ARE NOT AVAILABLE, USE LARGE (SEA) SCALLOPS and cut them in quarters before cooking them. If lobster is available and affordable, vary this salad by using 1 pound of diced cooked lobster meat in place of shrimp and scallops, eliminating the poaching steps.

DRESSING
¼ cup white-wine vinegar
½ teaspoon Crabtree & Evelyn Garlic & Parsley Mustard or Dijon-style mustard
½ teaspoon salt
  Pinch freshly ground black pepper
⅔ cup vegetable oil
3 tablespoons minced shallots
1 clove garlic, minced
1½ tablespoons minced fresh parsley
1 tablespoon minced fresh chervil, or 1 teaspoon dried

SALAD
¾ cup dry white wine
1 bay leaf
1 clove garlic, split
12 large shrimp
½ pound bay scallops
32 snow peas, stems and strings removed
4 cups shredded romaine
16 cherry tomatoes, halved
1½ tablespoons minced fresh parsley

TO SERVE
1 lemon, quartered

Alternatively, "cook" the shrimp and scallops in citrus juice for a wonderfully clear taste. In a shallow glass dish arrange the shellfish in 1 or 2 layers and cover them with fresh lemon and/or lime juice. Season with salt, pepper, garlic slivers, and a few onion slices. Cover the mixture with plastic wrap and chill it for several hours or overnight, turning the seafood to ensure that all surfaces lose their raw look and acquire the creaminess of cooked fish. Before serving, drain the seafood on paper towels, then dress and arrange it on the salad.

To make dressing, combine vinegar, mustard, salt, and pepper in a small bowl. Gradually add oil, whisking constantly until well incorporated. Add shallots, garlic, parsley, and chervil and blend well. Taste and correct seasoning, if necessary.

In a medium-sized, non-reactive saucepan, combine wine, bay leaf, garlic, and 1 cup water. Bring to a simmer over medium heat and simmer for 5 minutes. Meanwhile, remove shells from shrimp, leaving tails on, and devein them. Simmer shrimp gently in poaching liquid for about 2 minutes, or just until they turn bright pink. Using a slotted spoon, transfer shrimp immediately to a small bowl, let cool slightly, then spoon 3 tablespoons of dressing over them. Set aside to cool completely. Add scallops to poaching liquid and simmer for 30 seconds, or just until they turn white and opaque. Transfer immediately to a small plate and let cool (but without adding any dressing). When cool, cover shrimp and scallops and refrigerate separately.

Bring a large saucepan of water to a boil. Add snow peas and boil for 30 seconds. Turn peas into a colander and rinse under cold water to stop cooking and set color. Spread on a layer of paper towels to drain. Refrigerate until needed.

To assemble, add scallops to bowl with the shrimp. Add remaining dressing and toss to coat well. On a large serving platter or, for a picnic, in individual plastic containers with covers, make a bed of shredded romaine. Scatter snow peas on top. Remove shrimp and scallop mixture from dressing with a slotted spoon, reserving dressing, and spoon seafood over snow peas. Garnish with tomatoes and parsley.

Just before serving, drizzle reserved dressing over salad and garnish with lemon quarters.

— 4 SERVINGS —

Should you have access to scallops in the shell, serve the coral sections as well, treating them just as you would the creamy flesh.

*B*ASIL CORNBREAD

THIS BREAD MAY BE MADE EARLY IN THE DAY FOR AN EVENING MEAL, or in the evening for lunch the next day. Other herbs may be substituted for basil.

- ¼ cup (4 tablespoons) unsalted butter
- ⅔ cup all-purpose flour
- ⅔ cup yellow cornmeal
- 2 teaspoons baking powder
- ½ teaspoon salt
- ⅛ teaspoon freshly ground pepper
- 1 large egg
- ⅔ cup milk
- 2 tablespoons minced fresh basil, or 2 teaspoons dried

TO SERVE
Unsalted butter, softened

Preheat oven to 400 degrees F.

In a small saucepan, melt butter over very low heat. Remove from heat and let cool completely.

Sift flour, cornmeal, baking powder, salt, and pepper into a mixing bowl. In a small bowl, beat egg lightly, add milk, basil, and cooled butter, and stir into the flour mixture all at once until just blended.

Turn batter into a greased 8-inch-square baking dish and smooth top with a spatula. Bake in center of oven for 15 to 18 minutes, or until light golden and beginning to pull away from edges. Let cool completely. Serve cut into 2-inch squares, split horizontally, and buttered.

— MAKES SIXTEEN 2-INCH SQUARES —

CRUNCHY LEMON SYRUP CAKE

SERVE THIS CAKE WHILE IT'S STILL SLIGHTLY WARM, TOPPED WITH unsweetened whipped cream. It keeps for two to three days if kept in an airtight container.

1   cup all-purpose flour
¾   teaspoon baking powder
¼   teaspoon baking soda
    Pinch salt
4   tablespoons unsalted butter, softened
⅔   cup sugar
1   large egg (or 2 small eggs)
⅓   cup buttermilk or sour milk
1   tablespoon freshly grated lemon zest

    SYRUP
½   cup sugar
⅓   cup fresh lemon juice

Preheat oven to 350 degrees F.

Sift together flour, baking powder, baking soda, and salt and set aside.

In a large mixing bowl, cream together butter and sugar with an electric mixer or by hand until light and fluffy. Add egg and beat at high speed for 1 minute or vigorously by hand. Alternately add buttermilk and flour mixture in three additions, with mixer at low speed or stirring by hand. Stir in lemon zest.

Turn batter into a buttered and floured 8-inch springform pan, smoothing the top of batter with a spatula. Bake in the center of oven for 30 to 35 minutes, or until a skewer inserted into center of cake comes out clean.

Before cake is finished baking, in a saucepan combine sugar and lemon juice over low heat to make a syrup. Spoon syrup evenly over cake as it comes from the oven. Tip and rotate cake pan gently so that the syrup is distributed evenly over the surface of the cake.

Set cake, in its pan, on a wire rack to cool.

— 6 TO 8 SERVINGS —

This cake is also excellent when cooled, carefully sliced horizontally to form two layers, and filled with one of the Crabtree & Evelyn "fruit only" conserves.

SPORTING AFTERNOON

MENU

◆

*W*ILD MUSHROOM
BROTH

◆

*C*ORNISH HENS WITH
HONEY AND GINGER

◆

*O*RZO CONFETTI SALAD

◆

*G*RAPE TARTLETS
WITH ALMOND CRUST

OPPOSITE: WILD MUSHROOM BROTH,
CORNISH HENS WITH HONEY AND
GINGER, ORZO CONFETTI SALAD,
AND GRAPE TARTLETS WITH
ALMOND CRUST

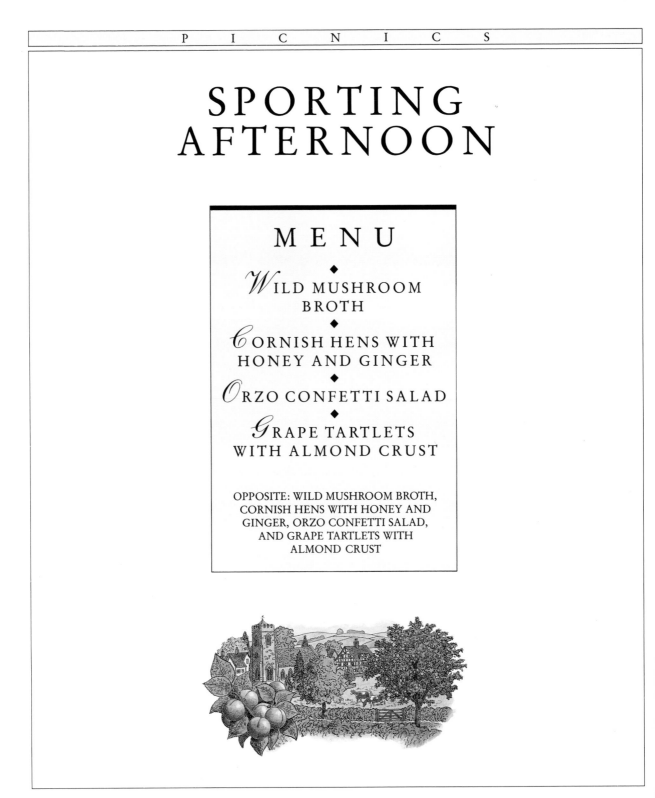

WILD MUSHROOM BROTH

THIS MAKES A BRACING THERMOS SOUP FOR A HIKE ON A COLD WINTER day. The better the quality of the beef stock, the more flavorful the soup. Any edible dried wild mushrooms can be used, but cèpes are among the most flavorful. If fresh herbs are not available for the bouquet garni, use ¼ teaspoon each of dried herbs.

6   cups beef stock
1½ ounces dried cèpes or other edible dried
     wild mushrooms
1   bouquet garni composed of 1 small bay leaf and
     1 fresh sprig each parsley, thyme, marjoram, and
     rosemary, all tied together with string
3   tablespoons Madeira or medium sherry
     Salt
     Freshly ground pepper

In a medium-sized saucepan, warm 2 cups of the stock over medium heat. Place mushrooms, rinsed, in a bowl, add warm stock, and let stand for 30 minutes.

Pour reconstituted mushrooms and their liquid back into the saucepan, being careful to hold back any dirt or sand that has settled to the bottom of the bowl. Add remaining 4 cups stock and bouquet garni and bring to a simmer over medium-low heat. Cover and simmer for 30 minutes.

Remove from heat and strain mixture through cheesecloth-lined sieve. When mushrooms are cool enough to handle, squeeze them in the cheesecloth to extract as much liquid as possible and discard mushrooms. Stir Madeira into stock, season with salt and pepper, if necessary, and serve hot.

— 4 SERVINGS —

To make a basic beef stock, in a kettle or large heavy saucepan combine ½ pound stewing beef and 1 pound beef bones, sawed into pieces by the butcher if necessary, with 1 onion, 1 leek, 1 carrot, ¼ small turnip, and a bouquet garni. Season with salt and pepper and a grating of nutmeg and add 2 quarts cold water.

Bring the water to a boil, skim off any froth that rises to the surface, and simmer the mixture for 1 to 1½ hours. Strain through a fine sieve and let cool.

Refrigerate until any fat solidifies on the surface. Remove the fat with a spoon before using the stock. The stock may be frozen.

CORNISH HENS WITH HONEY & GINGER

THIS SWEET, SPICY GLAZE IS AN EXCELLENT COMPLEMENT TO THE MILD flavors of the Cornish hen and to the pasta and vegetable salad. Serve the hens hot or at room temperature, and for easier handling on a picnic cut each in half.

2   Cornish hens
1   tablespoon olive oil
    Salt
    Freshly ground pepper
    GLAZE
⅓   cup Crabtree & Evelyn Honey & Ginger Sauce
1   tablespoon dry white wine
1   tablespoon white-wine vinegar
1   teaspoon Dijon-style mustard

Preheat oven to 400 degrees F.

Remove giblets from hens and reserve for another use. Rinse hens inside and out and pat dry. Using a large, heavy knife or cleaver, split hens in half through breastbones. Lay each hen flat and cut the meat away from the backbone, discarding backbones or reserving them with the giblets for a stock.

Brush hen halves with oil and season lightly with salt and pepper. Arrange hens, skin sides down, on a rack in a shallow roasting pan. Place pan in center of oven, reduce heat to 350 degrees F., and roast for 25 minutes.

Meanwhile, combine Honey & Ginger Sauce, wine, vinegar, and mustard in a small saucepan. Bring to a boil over medium-high heat, reduce heat to medium-low, and simmer for 2 minutes.

Remove hens from oven and brush generously with warm glaze. Turn hen halves skin sides up, brush skin generously with glaze, and return them to oven to bake for 30 minutes more, basting after 15 minutes with any remaining glaze and pan drippings. Hens are cooked when juices run clear when thigh meat is pierced at its thickest point with a knife.

— 4 SERVINGS —

The same honeyed piquancy can be given to cold chicken by mixing 2 to 4 tablespoons Crabtree & Evelyn Honey & Ginger Sauce into 1 cup mayonnaise and sharpening the mixture with a squeeze of lemon. This is also a perfect dressing for fruit and cottage cheese.

GRAPE TARTLETS WITH ALMOND CRUST

TAKE THESE TO A PICNIC IN THE PANS THEY WERE BAKED IN TO prevent crushing. Assemble them not more than 6 hours before serving time. For a single 10-inch tart, bake the crust for 15 minutes with the foil in and a further 20 to 30 minutes empty.

ALMOND CRUST
¼ cup slivered blanched almonds
1½ cups all-purpose flour
¼ teaspoon salt
3 tablespoons firmly packed brown sugar
½ cup (1 stick) cold unsalted butter, cut into small pieces
1 cold large egg
½ teaspoon vanilla extract
¼ teaspoon freshly grated lemon zest

GLAZE
¾ cup apricot preserves
3 tablespoons sherry

TO ASSEMBLE
¾ pound grapes, preferably an assortment of 2 or 3 colors, halved and, if necessary, seeded
¼ cup slivered blanched or unblanched almonds, lightly toasted

This rich nutty crust is a perfect pastry shell for spur-of-the-moment desserts, especially if the crusts are frozen uncooked in their pie plates, then thawed and cooked when needed. Fill with good-quality coffee ice cream and serve with Crabtree & Evelyn Honey & Ginger Sauce or with raspberry ice cream topped with Crabtree & Evelyn Blueberry Fruit Only Conserve.

Finely grind almonds in a food processor with on/off motion, or crush with a rolling pin until as finely ground as possible. Add flour, salt, and brown sugar to processor and blend, or combine ground almonds, flour, salt, and brown sugar in a bowl and stir to blend. Add butter and process or work with the fingertips until mixture resembles coarse crumbs.

In a small bowl beat egg lightly. Stir in the vanilla and lemon zest. With processor on, add egg mixture to dough through feed tube and process until dough forms, or add to mixing bowl, stirring constantly, and stir until dough forms. Pat dough into a ball, wrap in plastic wrap, and chill in refrigerator for at least 30 minutes.

Remove dough from refrigerator and divide into 8 equal pieces. Press each piece into a lightly buttered 3- to 3½-inch tartlet pan, preferably with removable rim, patting into an even layer. (The dough will soften as

you work with it.) Chill tartlet shells in freezer for at least 30 minutes before baking.

Preheat oven to 400 degrees F.

Remove tartlet shells from freezer, line each with a square of foil, and fill with pie weights or dried beans to prevent dough from puffing during baking. Bake on baking sheet in center of oven for 10 minutes. Remove foil with weights, reduce oven temperature to 350 degrees F., and continue baking for 15 to 20 minutes, or until pastry is a rich, golden brown. Let tartlet shells cool in pans for 10 minutes. Then carefully remove tartlet shells from pans and place on wire racks to cool completely.

To prepare glaze, combine preserves and sherry in a small saucepan and warm over medium heat, stirring, until preserves are melted. Strain through a sieve.

To assemble tarts, brush glaze on the bottom of each tartlet shell. Arrange grapes, cut sides down, in a decorative pattern, alternating colors, in the bottom of each pastry shell. Brush remaining glaze, reheating it if necessary, over grapes and edges of tartlets.

Sprinkle toasted almonds over tartlets before glaze sets. Serve at room temperature.

— MAKES EIGHT 3- TO 3½-INCH TARTLETS —

Open fruit tartlets or large tarts are among the prettiest summer desserts. For a strawberry or raspberry tart made with this crust, make a pastry cream based on the Cardamom Custard Sauce on page 242, but beat 4 tablespoons all-purpose flour into the egg yolk and sugar mixture and omit the cardamom.

When the half-and-half has been added, bring the custard to a simmer, then lower the heat and cook it, stirring, for 5 to 7 minutes. Add vanilla, let the mixture cool, and chill it, covered, until needed.

Assemble the tartlets or tart by spreading the pastry cream evenly over the fully baked almond crust. Arrange hulled strawberries or raspberries in concentric circles, stem ends down, over the pastry cream. Melt ½ cup red currant jelly with 1 teaspoon lemon juice and brush the glaze gently over the fruit.

ORZO CONFETTI SALAD

THIS IS A COLORFUL SALAD THAT CAN BE MADE WITH OTHER COMBINA-tions of diced raw and blanched vegetables. To serve the salad at a picnic, place the bowl or container of salad in the center of a platter surrounded with the endive and radicchio leaves, so that everyone can fill the leaves with salad and eat them with their fingers.

1½ cups uncooked orzo (rice-shaped pasta)
　　Salt

DRESSING
3　tablespoons white-wine vinegar
1　teaspoon Dijon-style mustard
6　tablespoons olive oil

⅓　cup finely chopped carrots
1　plum tomato, seeded and finely chopped
⅓　cup finely chopped sweet green pepper
⅓　cup finely chopped celery
⅓　cup finely chopped red onion
⅓　cup minced fresh parsley
　　Freshly ground black pepper
1　to 2 heads Belgian endive, leaves separated
1　to 2 heads radicchio, leaves separated

Bring a large saucepan of water to a boil over high heat. Add orzo and 1 tablespoon salt and boil for about 8 minutes, or until pasta is tender but still slightly firm. Turn orzo into a sieve, rinse under cold water to stop cooking, and drain well.

In a small bowl, combine vinegar and mustard, then whisk in oil. Bring a small saucepan of water to a boil over high heat, add carrots, and blanch for 2 minutes. Drain in a colander.

In a large bowl, combine orzo, carrots, tomato, green pepper, celery, onion, and parsley. Add dressing, season with salt and pepper, and toss to combine well. Serve with endive and radicchio.

— 4 TO 6 SERVINGS (ABOUT 6 CUPS) —

Pasta salads are light but nourishing warm-weather dishes, and the mixture of vegetables, meats, and fish can be a matter of choice. For an attractive effect, cut the meats and vegetables used approximately the same size and shape as the chosen pasta.

TRADITIONAL FRENCH

Shallot
~ WHITE ~
Wine Vinegar
7% ACETIC ACID

MATURED IN OAK CASKS

PRODUCED IN THE LOIRE VALLEY

250 ml 8.8 FL OZ

SUMMER'S TEA

M E N U

◆

ENGLISH GINGERBREAD

◆

CARDAMOM TOAST

◆

SALLY LUNN
(SEE APPENDIX)

◆

ALMOND TUILES

◆

CHOCOLATE PECAN
BREAD

◆

CHINA TEA AND INDIAN
TEA

OPPOSITE: ALMOND TUILES, ENGLISH
GINGERBREAD, AND SALLY LUNN

ℰNGLISH GINGERBREAD

MANY ENGLISH GINGERBREADS MUST MATURE FOR SEVERAL DAYS OR A week to achieve a rich, dark flavor and moistness. This recipe gives the traditional deep flavor but has a lighter texture and can be made as little as one day ahead. It also makes an excellent dessert, cut into larger pieces and served warm with whipped cream.

Ginger in its varied forms is versatile enough to contribute to every course of the meal, and so it is worth keeping the fresh, preserved, and ground root as staples in the kitchen. Gingerroot can also be potted, to become a large indoor plant with an exotic flower and an exquisitely sweet scent.

20 TEA BAGS

ASSAM

net wt 50 g 1.8 OZ

2½ cups flour
1½ teaspoons ground ginger
1 teaspoon ground cinnamon
½ teaspoon ground cloves
¼ teaspoon salt
½ cup (1 stick) butter
½ cup firmly packed dark brown sugar
½ cup molasses
½ cup dark corn syrup
1 teaspoon grated lemon zest
1 tablespoon freshly grated gingerroot
2 large eggs, beaten
2 teaspoons baking soda
1 cup boiling water
3 tablespoons powdered sugar

Preheat the oven to 350 degrees F.

In a large mixing bowl, sift the flour, ginger, cinnamon, cloves, and salt together and set aside.

In a small heavy saucepan, heat the butter, brown sugar, molasses, and corn syrup over low heat, stirring, until butter is melted and sugar dissolves. Remove from the heat, cool slightly, and stir in lemon zest and gingerroot.

Make a well in the center of dry ingredients and pour in the butter mixture and the eggs. Beat with a wooden spoon until smooth and well blended. In a small bowl, combine baking soda and boiling water and stir until dissolved. Pour over batter and stir gently until batter is well blended.

Pour batter into a 9-inch-square buttered and floured baking pan and bake in the center of the oven for 35 to 40 minutes, or until a toothpick inserted into the center comes out clean. Let cake cool in the pan. Dust the top with powdered sugar before cutting.

— MAKES 20 PIECES —

CARDAMOM TOAST

IF MAKING A LARGER QUANTITY, PUT THE SUGARED TRIANGLES OF toast in a very low oven while preparing the remaining pieces. Serve them warm, as they are, or with orange curd.

    2   tablespoons sugar
    ½   teaspoon ground cardamom
    4   slices firm white bread
        Unsalted butter, softened

Combine sugar and cardamom on a small plate and mix well.

Toast bread slices on both sides and butter both sides well. Cut each slice into 4 triangles. Gently press triangles into the cardamom sugar, coating both sides lightly. Arrange on a platter and serve warm.

— MAKES 16 TOAST TRIANGLES —

Serve these in a basket or warmed shallow dish lined with a cloth napkin to keep the toast warm and help retain the sweet spicy aroma that is released when the napkin is opened at the table.

ALMOND TUILES

THESE CLASSIC COOKIES ARE SHAPED TO RESEMBLE THE TILES (*TUILES*) on French rooftops. Bake only one sheetful at a time, as speed is of the essence when removing and shaping the cookies. They may, of course, simply be cooled flat on racks. But don't be afraid to try shaping them; it's a simple procedure that gives an impressive result.

EXTRA JAM
PEACH
P R E S E R V E
and
AMARETTO
with
ALMONDS

2 large egg whites	DECORATION
½ cup sugar	⅓ cup thinly sliced natural almonds
Pinch salt	
½ teaspoon vanilla extract	
½ teaspoon almond extract	
1½ tablespoons dark rum	
6 tablespoons flour	
4 tablespoons unsalted butter, melted and cooled	
⅓ cup finely chopped blanched almonds	

Preheat oven to 400 degrees F. Have ready a clean broom handle for shaping cookies.

In a mixing bowl, whisk the egg whites with the sugar, salt, vanilla and almond extracts, and rum until well blended. Stir in the flour and butter until smooth. Then add the chopped almonds. The batter should be very thin.

Drop the batter by teaspoonsful onto a large, well-buttered baking sheet, spacing them about 3 inches apart and baking only about 9 cookies at a time. With a small spatula, spread the batter evenly into very thin 2½-inch circles. Sprinkle each cookie with a few of the sliced almonds.

Bake in the center of the oven for 5 to 6 minutes, or until the edges are golden. Lay the broom handle across the backs of two chairs to give a rail for shaping the cookies. Remove cookies from the oven and, working quickly, lift warm cookies from the baking sheet with a spatula and drape them over the broom handle, curving the edges downward. (If the cookies become too cool to remove with ease from baking sheet, return them to the oven for about 30 seconds to soften.) Let cookies cool on the broom handle.

Bake remaining cookies in the same manner, re-buttering baking sheet between batches.

— MAKES ABOUT 36 COOKIES —

CHOCOLATE-PECAN BREAD

SERVE THIS BREAD IN THIN SLICES ARRANGED ON A SERVING DISH OR AS a whole loaf on a bread board, sliced as it is needed. Or serve with Cardamom Custard Sauce (page 242) poured around each slice on individual plates or passed separately in a sauceboat.

3	ounces semisweet chocolate	TO SERVE
1	tablespoon instant espresso powder	Powdered sugar
1	cup boiling water	
1½	cups flour	
2	teaspoons baking powder	
¼	teaspoon salt	
½	cup unsalted butter, softened	
1¼	cups granulated sugar	
2	large eggs	
1½	teaspoons vanilla extract	
½	cup coarsely chopped pecans	

Preheat oven to 350 degrees F.

Break or chop chocolate into small pieces and heat in the top of a double boiler over simmering water until melted. Set aside to cool completely. In a small bowl, dissolve espresso powder in the 1 cup boiling water and set aside to cool. Sift flour, baking powder, and salt onto a sheet of waxed paper and set aside.

Combine butter and sugar in a large mixing bowl and beat with an electric mixer or by hand until light and fluffy. Add eggs, one at a time, beating well after each addition, and beat in vanilla. Add chocolate and beat mixture on low speed, if using a mixer, until well blended. Stir in half the espresso mixture and half the flour mixture and blend well. Stir in remaining espresso mixture and remaining flour mixture and stir until blended. Stir in pecans.

Spoon batter into a 4- by 8½-inch buttered and floured loaf pan. Tap pan firmly to remove air pockets. Bake in the center of oven for 1 hour and 10 minutes, or until the top springs back when pressed lightly and a skewer inserted in the center comes out clean. Let cool in the pan for 10 minutes. Turn out onto a wire rack and let cool completely. Store in plastic wrap or an airtight container. Just before serving, sprinkle bread with powdered sugar.

— MAKES 12 TO 14 THIN SLICES —

NATURAL FLAVOUR

ALMOND Chocolate crisps

FROM Crabtree & Evelyn

net wt 175 g 6.2 OZ

For picnics, sandwich vanilla, chocolate, coffee, or orange icing between two slices of the pecan bread to make a dessert that is delicious and easier to transport than an iced cake.

SMASHING SERVICE

M E N U

◆

*W*ATERCRESS
SANDWICHES

◆

*R*ADISH FLOWER
SANDWICHES

◆

*R*ASPBERRIES AND
BLACKBERRIES WITH
RICOTTA CREAM

◆

*C*HOCOLATE
SHORTBREAD COOKIES

◆

*V*ICTORIA SPONGE

◆

*I*CED HERBAL TEA WITH
GERANIUM SUGAR

◆

*I*CED SPICED COFFEE

OPPOSITE: ICED HERBAL TEA WITH
GERANIUM SUGAR, WATERCRESS
SANDWICHES, AND RADISH FLOWER
SANDWICHES

WATERCRESS SANDWICHES

THE WATERCRESS BUTTER THAT IS PART OF THIS RECIPE CAN BE MADE IN advance and frozen.

WATERCRESS BUTTER
½ cup (1 stick) unsalted butter, softened
1 packed cup watercress leaves
1 teaspoon fresh lemon juice
¼ teaspoon freshly ground black pepper
  Pinch cayenne

16 thin slices of white bread
32 small watercress sprigs plus extra watercress for
  decoration

To make the watercress butter, in a food processor blend the butter, watercress leaves, lemon juice, black pepper, and cayenne until the mixture is very smooth. Let the mixture stand for about 30 minutes at room temperature (or chill it but bring it back to room temperature before using).

Spread each slice of bread with about 1½ teaspoons of the watercress butter, and cut 4 rounds from each slice with a 1½-inch round or fluted biscuit or canapé cutter. Arrange a watercress sprig on half the rounds, leaving a bit extending over the edge of each, and invert the remaining rounds on top to complete the sandwiches. Serve the sandwiches on a tray decorated with the extra watercress sprigs.

— MAKES 32 TEA SANDWICHES —

Although market water-cress is cultivated, the plant grows wild in streams in the U.S. and Europe. Wild watercress should, however, be used only if you are certain that the water where it grows is pure and that no animals, such as grazing sheep or cattle, drink from any part of the stream.

Watercress is usually kept fresh by standing the sprigs in a bowl of water, like a bouquet of flowers, in the re-frigerator. It will stay crisp and green longer, though, if the bunch is turned upside-down in the water, so that the leaves are submerged and the stems extend above the surface.

A pat of watercress but-ter enriches the flavor of simply broiled or grilled steak, chicken, and fish.

ℛADISH FLOWER SANDWICHES

½ cup (1 stick) unsalted butter, softened
1 tablespoon minced fresh chives
1 tablespoon minced flat-leaf parsley
1 tablespoon minced radish
   Salt
8 thin slices firm white bread, crusts removed

TO DECORATE
12 small radishes, very thinly sliced
   Fresh chive blades
   Fresh parsley sprigs
   Whole radishes for flowers (optional)

In a small bowl, combine butter, minced chives, minced parsley, and minced radish. Season with salt and beat until blended. Spread each bread slice with about 1 tablespoon of herb-radish butter. Cut each slice into 4 neat squares.

To decorate, place 2 radish slices, slightly overlapping, on each square. Place a chive blade at the bottom of each radish slice to form the stem for the flower, and place a sprig of parsley at the base of each chive blade to form a leaf.

Arrange on a platter, garnish platter with additional parsley sprigs and carved radish flowers, if desired, and serve. If not serving immediately, cover lightly and chill. Bring back to room temperature before serving.

— MAKES 32 TEA SANDWICHES —

The herbed radish butter can also be spread on the whole-wheat bread to add piquancy to roast beef, lamb, or fresh salmon sandwiches.

RASPBERRIES AND BLACKBERRIES WITH RICOTTA CREAM

This combination can also be used to fill individual tartlets: Shortly before serving, put a layer of the ricotta cream into each tartlet shell and arrange the fruit on top.

PURÉED AND FLAVORED RICOTTA MAKES A DELICIOUS AND UNUSUAL accompaniment to any juicy fruits.

1   pint red raspberries
1   pint blackberries
15 ounces whole-milk ricotta cheese (2 cups)
¼   cup powdered sugar
3   tablespoons Amaretto or Grand Marnier

Combine berries in a shallow serving dish.

Drain any excess liquid off ricotta. Purée in a food processor until smooth, add powdered sugar and Amaretto, and blend well. Spoon into a pretty serving dish and chill.

Pass berries and ricotta cream for guests to scoop spoonfuls of each, side by side, onto dessert plates.

— 8 SERVINGS (ABOUT 2 CUPS OF RICOTTA CREAM) —

$\mathcal{C}$HOCOLATE SHORTBREAD COOKIES

THESE COOKIES MAY BE CUT INTO MANY SHAPES BUT ARE PARticularly decorative cut out as hearts. The uncooked dough may be frozen and defrosted just before needed.

1   cup flour
½   cup unsweetened cocoa powder
½   cup powdered sugar
⅛   teaspoon salt
½   cup (1 stick) cold unsalted butter, cut into small
     pieces
1   large egg yolk
1   teaspoon vanilla extract
     Granulated sugar

Combine flour, cocoa powder, powdered sugar, and salt in a food processor or large mixing bowl and process or stir briefly to blend. Add butter and process about 30 seconds or rub in lightly with the fingertips until mixture resembles coarse crumbs. Add egg yolk and vanilla and process or stir until a smooth dough forms. Pat dough into a flattened ball, wrap in plastic wrap, and chill for at least 45 minutes.

Preheat oven to 325 degrees F.

On a lightly floured surface, roll out the dough about ¼ inch thick. Using a heart-shaped, scallop-edged, or other fancy cookie cutter, 1 to 2 inches in diameter, cut out cookies and place them 1 inch apart on lightly greased baking sheets. Sprinkle cookies with granulated sugar and bake in oven for 15 to 18 minutes, or until firm but not browned around the edges. Transfer cookies to a wire rack and let cool. Cooled cookies may be stored in an airtight container.

— MAKES 25 TO 30 COOKIES —

Shortbread has been a favorite sweet pastry in Scotland for centuries and was once included in several rites of passage there. In some areas a disk of the rich cookie would have been broken over a bride's head at her wedding, and a piece sewn into the hem of a baby's christening gown, each as a symbol of hope for their happiness and prosperity.

VICTORIA SPONGE

THIS SPONGE CAKE, A VERY SIMPLE, OLD-FASHIONED CAKE, IS A GREAT British favorite. Be sure to use a high-quality jam for the center. The cake will keep for a couple of days but is at its best fresh. If baked in advance, freeze the layers as soon as possible, then defrost and fill them only a few hours before serving.

¾ cup unsalted butter, softened
1 cup granulated sugar
3 large eggs
2 cups all-purpose flour
4 teaspoons baking powder
¾ cup strawberry or raspberry jam
2 tablespoons powdered sugar

Preheat the oven to 350 degrees F. Butter and flour two 8-inch round cake pans.

In a food processor cream the butter with the granulated sugar for 1 minute. With the motor running add the eggs, 1 at a time, processing for a further 5 seconds after each addition. Sift the flour and baking powder into the bowl of the food processor and pulse the mixture in short bursts several times to fold the dry ingredients into the butter mixture without overbeating it. The batter will be quite stiff.

Divide the batter between the 2 pans, gently smoothing the tops, and bake the cakes for 25 to 30 minutes, or until they spring back when lightly touched in the center. Let the cakes cool in the pans on racks for 10 minutes and then turn the layers out of the pans onto the racks to finish cooling.

To fill, spread 1 of the layers with the jam and top it with the second layer. Sift the powdered sugar over the top just before serving.

— SERVES 8 TO 10 —

*I*CED HERBAL TEA WITH GERANIUM SUGAR

ROSE AND LEMON GERANIUMS ARE PARTICULARLY SUITABLE FOR flavoring sugar and tea. A geranium tisane can be made by steeping scented geranium leaves (1 or 2 leaves per cup of hot water) with the tea.

2   to 3 scented geranium leaves
½   cup sugar
2   quarts herb tea
    Ice cubes

In a small bowl, bury geranium leaves in the sugar, cover the bowl, and let stand for 3 days.

Brew tea as usual and let steep to desired strength. Allow to cool. Pour into a pitcher filled with ice. Add geranium sugar as desired to flavor tea.

— MAKES 2 QUARTS —

*I*CED SPICED COFFEE

A STRONG BREW OF COFFEE IS NEEDED FOR THIS RECIPE, AS THE ICE cubes will melt and dilute it.

2   quarts fresh strong coffee
1   stick cinnamon
½   teaspoon ground nutmeg
10 pods cardamom, bruised
    Sugar

TO SERVE
Ice cubes
Heavy cream

Pour the freshly brewed hot coffee into a heatproof glass or Pyrex container. Add cinnamon, nutmeg, and cardamom and let cool. Cover and refrigerate for at least 4 hours. Strain coffee through a sieve and discard spices. Add sugar to taste, stirring until it is dissolved.

To serve, pour coffee into tall glasses filled with ice. Pass a pitcher of heavy cream separately.

— MAKES 2 QUARTS —

To keep ice cubes from diluting drinks, freeze tea, coffee, and fruit juices in ice cube trays and use these flavored cubes to cool the appropriate beverages.

CROQUET AND CUCUMBER SANDWICHES

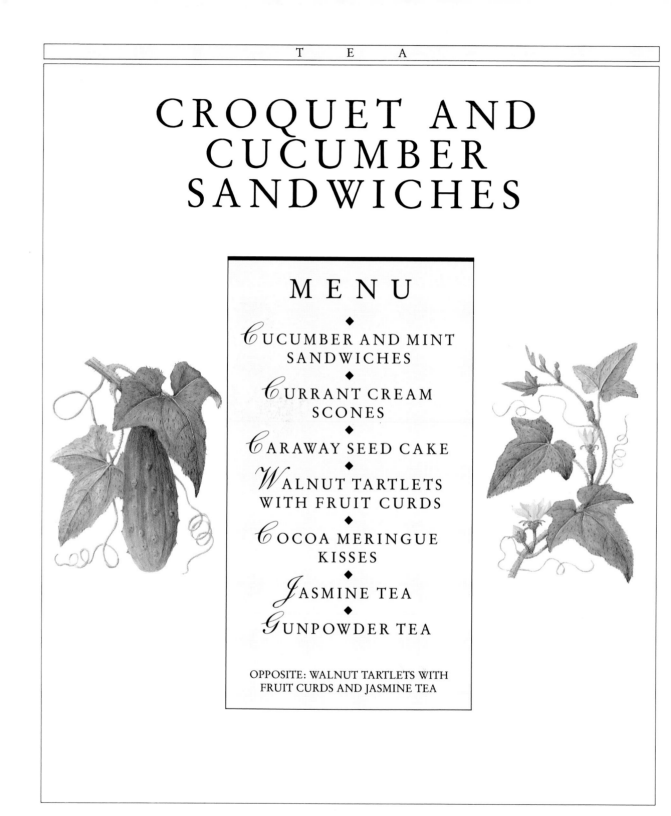

MENU

◆

Cucumber and Mint
Sandwiches

◆

Currant Cream
Scones

◆

Caraway Seed Cake

◆

Walnut Tartlets
with Fruit Curds

◆

Cocoa Meringue
Kisses

◆

Jasmine Tea

◆

Gunpowder Tea

OPPOSITE: WALNUT TARTLETS WITH
FRUIT CURDS AND JASMINE TEA

CUCUMBER AND MINT SANDWICHES

A REFRESHING VARIATION ON ONE OF ENGLAND'S MOST TRADITIONAL tea sandwiches, thinly sliced cucumber on good buttered bread. The crusts are always removed.

1 seedless cucumber	TO SERVE
32 small fresh mint leaves	Fresh mint sprigs
½ cup (1 stick) unsalted butter, softened	Thin orange slices
1 teaspoon grated orange zest	
8 thin slices firm white bread, crusts removed	
8 thin slices firm whole-wheat bread, crusts removed	

Peel the cucumber, halve lengthwise, and slice crosswise as thinly as possible. In a small bowl, combine mint leaves, butter, and orange zest and stir until creamy and blended.

Spread each slice of white bread with about 1½ teaspoons of the butter mixture. Arrange several slices of cucumber on each slice and top with the whole-wheat bread. Cut each sandwich into quarters to make 4 squares or triangles.

To serve, arrange sandwiches on a platter, alternating white and whole-wheat sides of sandwiches, and garnish with mint sprigs and orange slices.

— MAKES 32 TEA SANDWICHES —

CURRANT CREAM SCONES

SCONES MAY BE MADE EARLIER IN THE DAY AND REHEATED IN A 400 degree F. oven for 5 minutes before serving. They may also be frozen as soon as they have cooled after baking.

2 cups flour	6 tablespoons butter, cut into 10 pieces
2 teaspoons baking powder	¾ cup currants
2 tablespoons sugar	2 large eggs, well beaten
½ teaspoon salt	½ cup plus 1 tablespoon heavy cream

Preheat oven to 425 degrees F.

Sift flour, baking powder, 1 tablespoon of the sugar, and the salt into a mixing bowl. Add butter and work into flour mixture with the fingertips until mixture resembles coarse crumbs. Add currants and toss.

Keep a supply of mint butter in the freezer to use when fresh mint is out of season.

To make it, soften ½ pound (2 sticks) unsalted butter in a food processor and add 3 to 4 handfuls of clean, dry mint leaves. Process until smooth. Roll the butter into a log (or logs), wrap it in parchment paper, twisting the ends tightly, and freeze it. Slice the frozen mint butter into rounds as needed.

Make a well in flour mixture and add eggs and ½ cup of the cream. Mix with a wooden spoon until dough begins to clump together, then knead in the bowl for about 30 seconds; do not overwork dough.

Turn dough out onto a lightly floured surface and halve. Form each half into a ball and flatten to form a circle about ¾ inch thick and 5 inches in diameter. Cut each circle into 8 pie-shaped wedges. Place wedges about 1 inch apart on a lightly buttered baking sheet. Brush tops with remaining cream and sprinkle lightly with remaining sugar. Bake in the center of oven for 12 to 15 minutes, or until lightly browned.

Serve warm with raspberry or blackcurrant conserve.

— MAKES 16 SCONES —

Cocoa Meringue Kisses

3 large egg whites
¾ cup superfine sugar
4 teaspoons unsweetened cocoa powder
3 ounces semisweet chocolate

Preheat oven to 225 degrees F. Line 2 large baking sheets with parchment paper or butter and flour them lightly.

Beat egg whites in a bowl with an electric mixer at medium speed until very foamy and almost to the stage when soft peaks form. Add ½ cup of the sugar, 1 tablespoon at a time, beating at high speed after each addition, until a stiff, glossy meringue forms.

In a small bowl, sift together the cocoa powder and remaining sugar. Then sift this mixture over the meringue. Using a large spatula, gently but thoroughly fold the cocoa mixture into the meringue.

Spoon cocoa meringue into a pastry bag fitted with a star tip. Pipe 1-inch rosettes about 1 inch apart on baking sheets, lifting tip of pastry bag to form small points on the kisses.

Bake meringue kisses in the center of oven for about 2 hours, or until the bottoms are dry. Turn oven off and let kisses cool, or trans-transfer them to wire racks to cool.

Meanwhile, gently melt chocolate in a small saucepan over very low heat. When meringues are cooled, dip the top of each kiss into the chocolate and place the kisses on a wire rack to dry.

— MAKES ABOUT 60 KISSES —

CARAWAY SEED CAKE

THIS WONDERFULLY OLD-FASHIONED CAKE KEEPS FRESH IN AN AIR-tight container for several days and also freezes well. It looks handsome served unsliced on a cake stand or can be cut into thin pieces and arranged on a plate.

1⅓ cups flour
1   teaspoon baking powder
1   cup (2 sticks) unsalted butter, softened
1¼ cups plus 2 tablespoons granulated sugar
4   large eggs, separated
3   tablespoons whisky
3   tablespoons caraway seeds

TO SERVE
Powdered sugar

Preheat oven to 350 degrees F.

Sift flour and baking powder together onto a sheet of waxed paper. In a large mixing bowl, beat butter with 1¼ cups of the granulated sugar until mixture is light and fluffy. Add egg yolks and whisky and continue beating until smooth.

Gradually add flour mixture and caraway seeds to egg-butter mixture and continue beating until smooth.

In a separate bowl, beat egg whites until soft peaks form. Sprinkle in remaining 2 tablespoons granulated sugar and beat until whites are stiff but not dry.

Stir about ⅓ of the meringue into cake batter to lighten it. Gently fold in remaining meringue. Batter will remain quite stiff.

Spoon batter into a generously buttered 8-inch springform tube pan, lined on bottom with buttered parchment or waxed paper, and smooth the top. Bake in the center of oven for 50 to 55 minutes, or until cake pulls away from sides of pan and a toothpick inserted in center comes out clean. Let cool in the pan for 10 minutes. Turn out onto a wire rack and let cool completely.

Just before serving, sprinkle generously with powdered sugar.

— 10 TO 12 SERVINGS —

Walnut Tartlets with Fruit Curds

There are several sizes and shapes of molds available for making tiny, bite-size tartlets. When these small pastry shells are filled with different curds, in varying shades of yellow, the effect is very attractive. The dough can be made in advance and frozen.

1   cup flour
¼   cup ground walnuts
½   teaspoon salt
⅓   cup (5⅓ tablespoons) cold unsalted butter, cut into
    8 pieces
1¼ cups fruit curds, preferably of different flavors such
    as lemon and orange

TO SERVE
¼   cup finely chopped walnuts

Combine flour, ground nuts, and salt in a mixing bowl or the bowl of a food processor. Add butter and cut in by hand or process briefly until mixture resembles coarse crumbs. Sprinkle with 2 tablespoons cold water and toss with a fork or pulse quickly in processor. Add additional water by teaspoonsful, if needed, until dough is moist enough to hold together. Gather into a ball, flatten into a circle, and wrap in plastic wrap. Chill in the refrigerator for 45 minutes.

Preheat oven to 450 degrees F.

On a lightly floured surface, roll out dough about ⅛ inch thick. Cut dough to fit eighteen 1½- to 2-inch tartlet molds. Ease dough into the molds and press gently into corners and sides. Trim edges and prick surfaces with a fork. Chill tartlets on a baking sheet for about 20 minutes.

Bake tartlet shells in the center of oven for 8 to 10 minutes, or until lightly colored, and let cool slightly in molds. Carefully invert tartlet molds and let shells cool completely on a wire rack.

An hour or so before serving, spoon 1 to 2 teaspoons fruit curd into each pastry shell. Sprinkle the top of each with a few chopped walnuts.

— MAKES 18 TARTLETS —

English Country
Lemon
CURD
Made from
WHOLE EGGS
lemon juice,
Sugar & Butter.
Made in England

ENGLISH FARMHOUSE TEA

MENU

◆

*S*MITHFIELD HAM

◆

*P*OTTED SALMON

◆

*A*N ASSORTMENT OF
STUFFED EGGS

◆

*C*OTTAGE LOAF

◆

*W*HOLE-WHEAT SCONES

◆

*C*HEDDAR CHEESE

◆

*A*PPLE AND
RAISIN PIE

◆

*R*ICH CHOCOLATE
SQUARES

◆

*D*ARJEELING TEA

◆

*E*ARL GREY TEA

OPPOSITE: SMITHFIELD HAM, APPLE AND
RAISIN PIE, CHEDDAR CHEESE, COTTAGE
LOAF, WHOLE-WHEAT SCONES, HARD-
BOILED EGGS AND TINY TOMATOES
(NO RECIPE), POTTED SALMON, AND
RICH CHOCOLATE SQUARES

AN ASSORTMENT OF STUFFED EGGS

THE VARIETY OF FILLINGS FOR THESE EGGS PRODUCES A COLORFUL platter for any buffet. The eggs may be stuffed early in the day, arranged on the platter, loosely covered, and refrigerated.

For delicious egg salad sandwiches, season chopped hard-boiled eggs with any of the filling combinations and make up on whole-wheat or black bread.

24 medium eggs
1 large bunch fresh parsley

HAM AND WATERCRESS FILLING
6 tablespoons finely chopped ham, plus 6 tiny triangles ham for garnish
1½ tablespoons finely chopped watercress leaves
2 drops Tabasco or other hot pepper sauce
1 teaspoon Dijon-style mustard
¼ cup mayonnaise, or to taste
Salt
Freshly ground black pepper

DILL AND PARSLEY FILLING
1 tablespoon chopped fresh dill, or 1 teaspoon dried
2 tablespoons finely chopped fresh parsley
½ teaspoon Worcestershire sauce
2 tablespoons sour cream
2 tablespoons mayonnaise, or to taste
Salt
Freshly ground pepper
6 small sprigs fresh dill, or 6 flat-leaf parsley leaves

TOMATO AND HORSERADISH FILLING
2 teaspoons tomato paste
2 teaspoons prepared horseradish
¼ cup mayonnaise, or to taste
Salt
Freshly ground pepper
6 ¼-inch strips tomato

CURRY AND SHALLOT FILLING
1 teaspoon finely chopped shallot
1 teaspoon curry powder
2 tablespoons sour cream
2 tablespoons mayonnaise, or to taste
Salt
Coarsely ground pepper

Place eggs in a large saucepan and add enough cold water to cover. Bring to a boil, covered, over medium-high heat, remove from heat, and let stand, covered, for about 20 minutes. Drain eggs, rinse well under cold water, and peel. Let cool completely.

Discard stems from parsley. Arrange bed of parsley sprigs on a large platter and chill in the refrigerator while preparing fillings.

To prepare ham and watercress filling, cut 6 of the eggs in half lengthwise and carefully remove yolks. Set whites aside. Place yolks in a small mixing bowl, add chopped ham, watercress, Tabasco, mustard, and mayonnaise, and mash with a fork until blended and smooth. (Add more mayonnaise if needed to make a smooth paste.) Season lightly with salt and pepper and blend. Spoon filling into a pastry bag fitted with a star tip and pipe into the hollows of the whites. Garnish each egg with a triangle of ham. Chill, covered.

To prepare dill and parsley filling, cut 6 of the remaining eggs in half lengthwise and carefully remove yolks. Set whites aside. Place yolks in a small mixing bowl, add dill, parsley, Worcestershire sauce, sour cream, and mayonnaise, and mash with a fork until blended and smooth. (Add more mayonnaise if needed to make a smooth paste.) Season lightly with salt and pepper and blend. Spoon filling into a pastry bag fitted with a star tip and pipe into the hollows of the whites. Garnish each egg with a dill sprig or parsley leaf. Chill, covered.

To make tomato and horseradish filling, cut 6 of the remaining eggs in half lengthwise and carefully remove yolks. Set whites aside. Place yolks in a small mixing bowl, add tomato paste, horseradish, and mayonnaise, and mash with a fork until blended and smooth. (Add more mayonnaise if needed to make a smooth paste.) Season lightly with salt and pepper and blend. Spoon filling into a pastry bag fitted with a star tip and pipe into the hollows of the whites. Garnish each egg with a strip of tomato. Chill, covered.

To make curry and shallot filling, cut remaining 6 eggs in half lengthwise and carefully remove yolks. Set whites aside. Place yolks in a small mixing bowl, add shallot, curry powder, sour cream, and mayonnaise, and mash with a fork until blended and smooth. (Add more mayonnaise if needed to make a smooth paste.) Season lightly with salt and pepper and blend. Spoon filling into a pastry bag fitted with a star tip and pipe into the hollows of the whites. Garnish each egg with a generous grinding of coarse pepper. Chill.

To serve, arrange eggs on the bed of parsley.

— MAKES 48 STUFFED EGGS —

To ensure that the eggs will not crack while boiling, add 2 tablespoons vinegar or salt to the water. Peeling the eggs as soon as they are cool enough to handle makes the whites come away from the shells more easily, and eggs that are several days old peel better than do freshly laid ones.

COTTAGE LOAF

THIS ENGLISH COUNTRY LOAF IS TRADITIONALLY SHAPED IN THE FORM of a large bun with a knob on top. The dough is easy to make and can be shaped and baked in smaller rolls as well.

2¾ to 3 cups flour
1   teaspoon salt
½   teaspoon sugar
1   ¼-ounce package quick-rising yeast
⅔   cup milk
1   tablespoon butter

In a large mixing bowl or the bowl of a heavy-duty mixer, combine 2 cups of the flour with the salt, sugar, and yeast.

In a small saucepan, combine milk, butter, and ½ cup water and warm over low heat until butter is melted and the liquid feels hot (125 to 130 degrees F.). Pour liquid into dry ingredients and stir with a wooden spoon to make a coarse dough.

Knead by hand for about 8 minutes, adding as much additional flour as is needed to make a smooth, elastic dough.

Turn dough into a large buttered bowl, turning it to coat all sides. Cover bowl loosely with a damp towel and set aside to rise in a warm place for about 45 minutes, or until dough is double in bulk. Punch dough down, knead for about 2 minutes, and cover and set aside for 30 minutes more, until double in bulk again.

Punch dough down. Break off about one-quarter of the dough, shape into a small ball, and set aside. Shape remaining dough into a large ball and place in the middle of a buttered baking sheet. Place smaller ball on top of the large ball and insert forefinger down through the center of both balls until finger touches the baking sheet. Let rise for 30 minutes. Meanwhile, preheat oven to 450 degrees F.

Bake loaf in the center of oven for 10 minutes. Reduce heat to 375 degrees F. and bake for 25 to 30 minutes longer, or until the top is golden brown and the loaf sounds hollow when thumped lightly on the bottom. Let cool on a wire rack.

— MAKES 1 LOAF —

This shape can also be used for individual rolls by dividing the dough into 18 equal pieces and forming tiny cottage loaves from each. Bake these at 425 degrees F. for about 20 minutes.

$\mathcal{P}$OTTED SALMON

SPREAD THIS MIXTURE ON SCONES, SLICES OF COTTAGE LOAF, OR ON toast for teatime. It should be chilled for several hours, but take it from the refrigerator about an hour before serving to allow it to soften to a spreading consistency.

1 cup dry white wine
1 bay leaf
  Pinch ground nutmeg
  Salt
6 peppercorns
1 pound fillet of salmon, preferably cut from the tail
½ cup (1 stick) unsalted butter
2 teaspoons minced fresh dill, or ½ teaspoon dried
  Freshly ground pepper
  Fresh dill or parsley sprigs

In a small, non-reactive saucepan just large enough to hold the salmon, combine wine, bay leaf, nutmeg, ¼ teaspoon salt, and peppercorns. Bring to a simmer and cook for 5 minutes. Add salmon and a tablespoon or so water, or enough for liquid to just cover the fish. Bring to a simmer over medium heat, reduce heat to low, and poach for 8 to 10 minutes, or until the fish just loses its translucency. Transfer salmon with a slotted spatula to a plate and let it cool. Discard the bay leaf and peppercorns and simmer poaching liquid over medium heat until it is reduced to about 2 tablespoons. Set aside.

In a small saucepan, melt 2 tablespoons of the butter over low heat, skimming off any foam that rises to the top, and set aside to allow milky solids to settle in the bottom.

Remove and discard skin, any small bones, and very dark meat from the salmon. Flake fish into the bowl of a food processor. Cut remaining 6 tablespoons butter into pieces and add to the food processor, along with the minced dill and reduced poaching liquid. Process with short on/off pulses in order to retain some of the salmon's texture. Season with salt and pepper, if desired.

Pack salmon mixture into a crock and smooth the top with a spatula. Lay small sprigs of dill or parsley on top and spoon a thin layer of the clarified butter over the top. Refrigerate for several hours.

— MAKES ABOUT 2 CUPS —

Potted salmon, served from the crock or—for more formal meals—in individual ramekins, also makes a fine first course at lunch or dinner. Serve it with strips of warm toast and wedges of lemon. Slightly more clarified butter may be needed to cover the salmon if it is potted in individual dishes.

Whole-Wheat Scones

EAT THESE SCONES WARM FROM THE OVEN, SPREAD WITH POTTED Salmon (page 149) or an assortment of good preserves.

2	cups whole-wheat flour
2½	teaspoons baking powder
½	teaspoon salt
6	tablespoons cold unsalted butter, cut into 10 pieces
1	large egg
½	cup milk

Preheat oven to 425 degrees F.

Sift flour, baking powder, and salt into a large bowl, adding any whole-wheat flakes that don't pass through the sifter into the bowl. Add butter and work it into the flour mixture with the fingertips until the mixture has a grainy texture.

In a small bowl, combine egg and milk and beat together lightly. Make a well in the center of flour mixture, pour in egg mixture, and stir with a wooden spoon until a dough begins to form. Knead dough in the bowl about 15 times, or until it is just smooth.

Turn dough out onto a lightly floured surface and knead 3 to 4 times,

Some cooks are convinced that the extra lightness of their scones results from rubbing the butter into the flour while lifting the ingredients into the air above the bowl and letting them fall—thus introducing more air into the mixture.

then form into a circle about ¾ inch thick. Transfer dough to a lightly buttered baking sheet. Using a sharp knife, make a deep cut across the round without slicing all the way through to the baking sheet. Make a second cut at right angles to the first to form 4 quarters. Then mark each quarter into 3 equal wedges to form 12 wedge-shaped scones.

Bake in the center of the oven for 15 to 18 minutes, or until lightly browned.

— MAKES 12 SCONES —

While these scones are best eaten within a few hours of baking, they freeze well. Reheat by placing them, still frozen, in a 300 degree F. oven for about 10 minutes.

$\mathscr{R}$ICH CHOCOLATE SQUARES

SERVE THESE MOIST, FLAVORFUL SQUARES PLAIN OR, FOR THE TRUE chocolate addict, ice them with chocolate frosting.

½ cup (1 stick) butter	1 teaspoon vanilla extract
4 ounces unsweetened chocolate	1 cup flour
4 large eggs	
Pinch salt	TO SERVE
1½ cups granulated sugar	Powdered sugar

Preheat oven to 350 degrees F.

In a medium saucepan or in the top of a double boiler, melt butter and chocolate over low heat or simmering water. Remove from the heat and let cool to lukewarm.

Meanwhile, beat eggs and salt in a mixing bowl with an electric mixer for about 2 minutes, or until mixture is light and double in volume. Gradually add sugar, beating constantly. Beat in the vanilla. Gradually add the chocolate mixture, beating on low speed. Sift the flour over the mixture and stir with a wooden spoon just until flour is incorporated and no white specks remain.

Turn batter into a buttered 9-inch-square baking pan. Bake in the center of oven for 30 minutes, or until a shiny crust forms and edges pull away from the pan. Center should still be moist when tested with a toothpick.

Let cool in the pan on a wire rack. Cut into 36 squares, dust with powdered sugar, and arrange on a platter to serve.

— MAKES 36 SMALL SQUARES —

NATURAL FLAVOUR

RASPBERRY

Chocolate crisps

FROM Crabtree & Evelyn

net wt 175 g 6.2 OZ

APPLE AND RAISIN PIE

PASTRY

2½	cups flour
2	teaspoons sugar
½	teaspoon salt
¾	cup (1½ sticks) cold unsalted butter, cut into pieces
2	tablespoons cold solid vegetable shortening, cut into pieces

FILLING

6	firm tart apples, such as Granny Smith
¾	cup raisins
¾	cup firmly packed brown sugar
¼	teaspoon ground nutmeg
½	teaspoon grated lemon zest
½	teaspoon grated orange zest
1	tablespoon fresh lemon juice
1	teaspoon vanilla extract
1	tablespoon flour
2	tablespoons butter, cut into pieces

This filling can also be used as the heart of a winter apple crisp. Mix the ingredients together, put them into a 1½-quart ovenproof dish, and top with a crumble of 1½ cups crushed oats lightly mixed with 6 tablespoons melted butter and ⅓ cup light brown sugar. Bake at 350 degrees F. for about 1 hour, or until the juices bubble up around the edges of the topping and the fruit is softened.

To make pastry, combine flour, sugar, and salt in the bowl of a food processor and pulse with on/off motion to mix. Add butter and shortening and pulse until pieces of fat are the size of lima beans. Add ⅓ cup ice water through the feed tube, pulsing with on/off motion until dough begins to clump together. If necessary, add additional ice water by teaspoons until dough forms. Turn dough out onto a lightly floured surface and form into 2 circles, one slightly larger than the other. Wrap the smaller one in plastic wrap and chill. Roll remaining dough out into a 10-inch round and fit it into a 9-inch pie pan. (Do not trim edge.) Cover with plastic wrap and chill for at least 30 minutes.

Preheat oven to 375 degrees F.

Peel, core, and thinly slice apples. In a mixing bowl toss them with the raisins, brown sugar, nutmeg, lemon zest, orange zest, lemon juice, vanilla, and flour, turn mixture into the chilled pastry shell, and dot the top with butter.

Roll out remaining dough into a 9½-inch round and place it over filling. Press pastry edges firmly together and trim. Crimp edges with the fingertips or the tines of a fork to seal and then cut slashes in the top crust to allow steam to escape. Bake in the center of oven for 45 to 55 minutes, or until the crust is golden and the filling bubbly.

— MAKES ONE 9-INCH PIE —

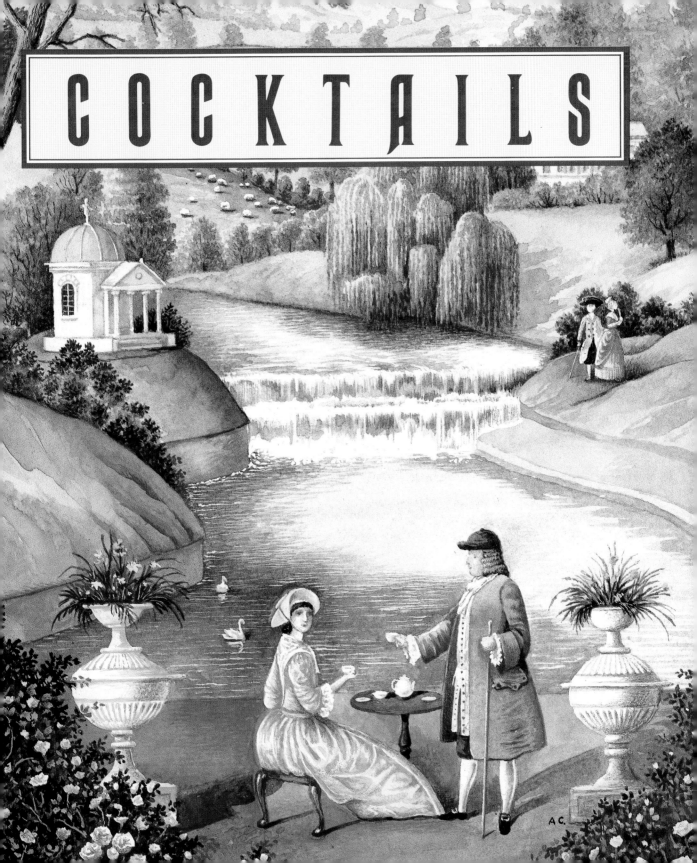

COCKTAILS

GARDEN PARTY

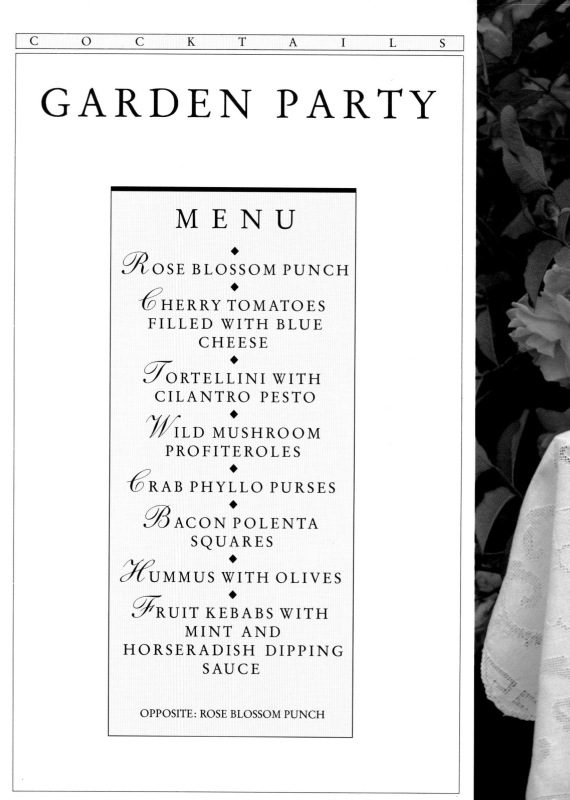

MENU

◆

*R*OSE BLOSSOM PUNCH

◆

*C*HERRY TOMATOES
FILLED WITH BLUE
CHEESE

◆

*T*ORTELLINI WITH
CILANTRO PESTO

◆

*W*ILD MUSHROOM
PROFITEROLES

◆

*C*RAB PHYLLO PURSES

◆

*B*ACON POLENTA
SQUARES

◆

*H*UMMUS WITH OLIVES

◆

*F*RUIT KEBABS WITH
MINT AND
HORSERADISH DIPPING
SAUCE

OPPOSITE: ROSE BLOSSOM PUNCH

ROSE BLOSSOM PUNCH

THIS LIGHT, FRESH-TASTING DRINK LOOKS STUNNING SERVED FROM A clear punch bowl. A rose-filled block of ice floating in the punch keeps it chilled at serving time but must be made at least a day ahead.

3 pink unsprayed roses, with
   about 6-inch stems, rinsed
8 cups dry white wine, chilled
½ cup Kirsch
1 to 2 tablespoons rosewater

TO SERVE
Small pink unsprayed rose petals
and leaves, rinsed and patted dry

The day before you plan to serve the punch, prepare the rose-filled ice cube for the center of the punch bowl. To do so, thoroughly rinse out a half-gallon cardboard milk or juice carton with water. Cut off top and trim top of sides to about 7 inches. Place roses in carton. Fill to within 1 inch of top with boiled and cooled water. Freeze overnight, or until solidly frozen.

To make the punch, combine wine, Kirsch, and rosewater in a wide glass punch bowl. Remove cardboard from the rose-studded ice cube and place cube in the center of punch bowl. Float small rose petals and leaves on top of punch. Serve punch in clear, long-stemmed wineglasses.

— 16 SERVINGS —

CHERRY TOMATOES FILLED WITH BLUE CHEESE

THE MILDNESS OF DANISH BLUE CHEESE MARRIES WELL WITH TART tomatoes, whereas the stronger flavor of Stilton is delicious with sweeter varieties of tomato.

25 small cherry tomatoes,
   stems removed

FILLING
4 ounces Danish blue cheese or
   Stilton cheese
½ cup cream cheese

2 tablespoons heavy cream
2 tablespoons grated onion

TO ASSEMBLE
Salt
Freshly ground pepper
Snipped chives

Cut tomatoes in half horizontally and carefully scoop seeds out of each half with a demitasse spoon or small melon-ball cutter. Place scooped out halves upside-down on paper towels to drain.

Combine blue cheese, cream cheese, cream, and onion in a mixing bowl or food processor and beat with an electric mixer or process until thoroughly blended.

Invert tomato halves and sprinkle cavities lightly with salt and pepper. Spoon cheese mixture into a pastry bag fitted with a star tip and pipe it into each tomato half. Garnish with chives and arrange on a platter.

— MAKES 50 HORS D'OEUVRES —

$\mathcal{T}$ORTELLINI WITH CILANTRO PESTO

THE SAUCE, WHICH CAN BE MADE IN ADVANCE, OWES ITS INSPIRATION to *pesto genovese*, the classic Ligurian mixture of basil, pine nuts, olive oil, and sardo cheese.

CILANTRO PESTO
- ¼ cup dry roasted peanuts
- 1 shallot, quartered
- 1 cup packed flat-leaf parsley leaves
- ¾ cup packed fresh cilantro leaves
- ¾ cup light olive oil

- 2 tablespoons red-wine vinegar
  Salt
  Freshly ground pepper

PASTA
- ½ pound fresh cheese-stuffed egg tortellini
- ½ pound fresh cheese-stuffed spinach tortellini

Bring a large pot of salted water to a boil.

Meanwhile, in a food processor pulse peanuts, shallot, parsley, and cilantro with an on/off motion to produce a coarse paste. With the motor on, drizzle oil and vinegar through the feed tube. Add salt and pepper to taste and process briefly to blend.

Add tortellini to boiling water, let water return to a boil, and cook for 5 to 8 minutes, or until pasta is tender but still slightly firm, or *al dente*.

Drain pasta in a colander and return it to pot. Add sauce and toss gently to coat pasta well.

To serve, turn pasta into a shallow serving bowl or platter. Pass along with a small glass of toothpicks for spearing and eating the pasta. Serve warm or tepid.

— 8 COCKTAIL SERVINGS —

This green sauce also flavors chicken wonderfully. Slip the fingers under the skin on the breast of a roasting chicken to form a large pocket on either side of the breastbone. Spoon the sauce into the pockets and rub the outside of the skin to spread the mixture evenly.

Roast the chicken in the usual way. Every slice of white meat will have a sliver of the aromatic seasoning, and if there is a spoonful or so left over, stir this into the gravy. Half-quantities are adequate for a 6-pound chicken.

WILD MUSHROOM PROFITEROLES

THE PASTRY PUFFS SHOULD BE FILLED JUST BEFORE SERVING, BUT BOTH the puffs and the filling can be made early in the day and reheated. Reheat the pastry puffs in a 300 degree F. oven for a few minutes until re-crisped. Heat the filling gently in a saucepan set over hot water before spooning or piping into pastry puffs.

1 ounce dried wild mushrooms such as cèpes, porcini, or morels (see Note)

CHOUX PASTRY
4 tablespoons unsalted butter
Salt
Freshly ground white pepper
1 cup flour
4 large eggs

MUSHROOM FILLING
½ pound cultivated, white mushrooms
3 tablespoons unsalted butter
2 large shallots, minced
2 tablespoons chopped fresh tarragon, or 2 teaspoons dried
½ cup heavy cream
Pinch freshly grated nutmeg
1 to 2 teaspoons fresh lemon juice
1 tablespoon chopped flat-leaf parsley
Salt
Freshly ground pepper

TO FINISH
40 whole flat-leaf parsley leaves

Brush away any dirt that clings to the wild mushrooms and place them in a small bowl. Add enough boiling water to cover and set aside to soak for 30 minutes.

Meanwhile, prepare the *choux* pastry: Preheat oven to 400 degrees F. In a heavy saucepan, combine butter with ½ cup water and season with a pinch each of salt and white pepper. Bring to a rolling boil, reduce heat to low, and add flour all at once, stirring vigorously until mixture pulls away from the side of the pan and forms a ball. Remove from the heat and let cool slightly. Add 3 of the eggs, one at a time, beating vigorously for 1 to 2 minutes after each addition until batter becomes smooth and satiny. In a small bowl beat remaining egg with 1 teaspoon water to form an egg wash and set aside.

Drop the batter by teaspoonsful about 2 inches apart onto lightly buttered baking sheets to form small mounds or spoon batter into a pastry bag fitted with a plain ⅜-inch tip and pipe mounds onto baking sheets. (Mounds should be about ¾ inch in diameter.) Brush the tops of the mounds lightly with the egg wash. Bake in the center of the oven for 15 to 20 minutes, or until rounds are puffed, golden brown, and hollow in the middle. Let cool on wire racks.

To prepare the filling, turn the wild mushrooms into a sieve lined with a double layer of cheesecloth set over a small saucepan to catch the soaking liquid. Thoroughly rinse mushrooms, removing any remaining dirt or debris, and place in the bowl of a food processor. Place the saucepan with mushrooms' soaking liquid over medium heat and simmer until reduced to about 2 tablespoons.

Add cultivated mushrooms to the wild mushrooms in the food processor and pulse with on/off motion until all are finely chopped.

In a large skillet, melt the butter over medium-low heat, add shallots, and cook for 1 minute. Add mushrooms, their reduced liquid, and the tarragon. Cook over medium heat, stirring frequently, until all liquid has evaporated, approximately 5 minutes. Stir in cream and nutmeg and simmer over low heat, stirring frequently, for about 15 minutes, or until the cream is entirely absorbed by the mushrooms. Season with lemon juice, chopped parsley, salt, and pepper and keep mixture warm.

To assemble, make a small split on the side of each pastry puff and spoon about 1 teaspoon of the filling into the center. Arrange a parsley leaf on the filling of each puff so that it extends over the edge of the puff, pat the tops in place, and arrange the puffs on a platter.

— MAKES ABOUT 40 PROFITEROLES —

Note: If fresh wild mushrooms are available, substitute 5 ounces of them for the 1 ounce of dried mushrooms.

This filling is delicious and versatile. For a change, spread it thickly on fingers of white toast, keeping it a bit in the middle. Broil the toast fingers for 2 to 3 minutes, or until the mushroom mixture is heated through, and serve them as hors d'oeuvres. The filling can also be used in savory crêpes, or it can be spooned into large mushroom caps that have first been lightly sautéed. Broil the stuffed mushrooms for about 5 minutes, so that the filling is hot but the caps are not overcooked.

CRAB PHYLLO PURSES

Phyllo sheets are a great ally to the cook, whether assembled in the traditional streudel form or in bite-size purses.

PHYLLO PASTRY IS EASY TO HANDLE AS LONG AS THE STACK OF UNUSED sheets is kept covered with a damp kitchen towel to prevent drying while the purses are being assembled. The purses may be prepared to the point of baking, then frozen in a single layer on the baking sheet. If baking them from the frozen state, add about 5 minutes to the cooking time.

¾ cup (1½ sticks) unsalted butter
6 tablespoons minced green onion
2 tablespoons dry vermouth
4 teaspoons Dijon-style mustard
4 tablespoons minced parsley
2 tablespoons minced fresh dill, or 2 teaspoons dried
4 drops Tabasco or other hot chili sauce
¼ teaspoon Worcestershire sauce
½ pound fresh crab meat
¼ cup *crème fraîche* or sour cream
Salt
Freshly ground pepper
6 sheets phyllo pastry dough (12 by 16 inches each)
¼ cup dry bread crumbs
1 tablespoon freshly grated Parmesan cheese

Fillings should be reasonably firm and can include fish, meat, or vegetable mixtures as well as fruit combinations for pies.

Melt ½ cup (1 stick) of the butter in a small saucepan over very low heat and set aside.

Melt remaining 4 tablespoons butter in a medium skillet, add green onions, and cook over medium-low heat until softened, about 3 minutes. Stir in vermouth and mustard and cook, stirring, about 2 minutes. Add parsley, dill, Tabasco, Worcestershire sauce, crab meat, and *crème fraîche*. Season with salt and pepper and stir to blend thoroughly. Remove from the heat and let cool to room temperature.

Preheat oven to 375 degrees F.

Spread phyllo sheets out on a flat surface between 2 slightly damp kitchen towels. In a small bowl, combine bread crumbs and cheese.

Carefully remove one sheet of phyllo and place on another damp towel on a flat surface (re-covering remaining phyllo), brush it with melted butter, then sprinkle lightly with some of the bread crumb mixture. Fold phyllo in half to form an 8- by 12-inch rectangle. Brush again with butter. Using a sharp knife, cut phyllo into six 4-inch squares. Mound about 1½ teaspoons crab meat filling in the center of each square. Then carefully gather up edges of squares with your fingers and pinch together in the centers to form plump "purses." Brush the centers and edges with butter to prevent drying and cracking and place purses on a lightly buttered baking sheet. Repeat the procedure with remaining 5 phyllo sheets and bread crumb mixture, to make 36 purses.

Bake in center of oven for 12 to 15 minutes, or until lightly golden and crisp. Transfer to wire racks to cool slightly.

Serve warm or at room temperature.

— MAKES 36 HORS D'OEUVRES —

FRUIT KEBABS WITH MINT AND HORSERADISH DIPPING SAUCE

THIS RECIPE REQUIRES THE BEST OF THE SUMMER'S RIPE FRUITS. THE greater the variety of fruit used, the more colorful and attractive this presentation will be.

100	to 120 cubes of fresh summer fruits such as cantaloupe, watermelon, honeydew, peaches, kiwi, and strawberries
30	wooden skewers (6 inches long)
¾	cup heavy cream
3	tablespoons chopped fresh mint leaves
2	teaspoons freshly grated horseradish or well-drained bottled horseradish

TO SERVE
2   large bunches fresh mint

Thread 3 or 4 cubes of different types and colors of fruit onto each of the wooden skewers.

In a small bowl, beat cream just until soft peaks form and fold in chopped mint and horseradish. Pour dipping sauce into a serving bowl that is shallow and wide enough for fruit skewers to be dipped lengthwise.

Arrange a bed of mint sprigs on a basket or large tray and pile fruit skewers attractively on mint. Or stick skewers into a cantaloupe or watermelon half in the center of a round platter decorated with mint sprigs. Serve fruit skewers with sauce.

— MAKES 30 HORS D'OEUVRES —

Fruit cubes on skewers with a bowl of whipped cream sugared to taste and sharpened with rum makes a light, simple dessert for informal meals throughout the year.

BACON POLENTA SQUARES

The chilled polenta can also be cut into 2-inch rounds arranged in overlapping circles in a fairly shallow round baking dish, sprinkled with grated cheese, and baked as for the squares. Serve with a mushroom or tomato sauce, accompanied by a green salad and French bread.

8	ounces bacon
1½	cups yellow cornmeal
1	teaspoon salt
¾	teaspoon freshly ground pepper
	Pinch ground nutmeg
2½	cups grated sharp Cheddar cheese (10 ounces)
4	teaspoons finely chopped fresh thyme leaves, or 1½ teaspoons dried

TO SERVE
Fresh thyme sprigs

In a large skillet, sauté bacon over medium heat until crisp. Drain on paper towels. Crumble bacon and set aside.

Fill a large heavy saucepan with 3 cups water and bring to a boil. Meanwhile, place cornmeal in a bowl with 2½ cups water and stir to blend well. Stir moistened cornmeal into boiling water, reduce heat to medium-low, and cook, stirring almost constantly with a wooden spoon, for 20 minutes, or until mixture is very thick and begins to pull away from the side of the pan. Remove from heat and stir in salt, pepper, nutmeg, bacon, 1 cup of the cheese, and 2 teaspoons of the thyme leaves.

While still warm, pour polenta mixture into a well-buttered 10- by 5-inch jelly-roll pan or rimmed baking sheet. Spread mixture out as evenly as possible with a rubber spatula and smooth the top. (Polenta should be about ¼ inch thick.) Set aside to cool to room temperature. Then chill in the refrigerator until firm and set, at least 1 hour. (If not baking immediately, cover polenta with plastic wrap when chilled and set.)

Preheat oven to 400 degrees F.

Sprinkle remaining 1½ cups cheese and 2 teaspoons thyme leaves over top of chilled polenta. Bake in center of oven for 25 to 30 minutes, or until cheese is melted and bubbly and the polenta is beginning to brown around the edges. Remove from oven and let cool in the pan for 10 minutes before cutting. Cut into 5 equal strips lengthwise and 10 across.

To serve, arrange in a napkin-lined basket or tray, garnish with thyme sprigs, and serve warm.

— MAKES 50 HORS D'OEUVRES —

Hummus with Olives

FRESHLY COOKED DRIED CHICK PEAS PRODUCE THE BEST FLAVOR BUT must be soaked in water to cover by 3 inches and chilled overnight before cooking. Good canned chick peas may be substituted. Crudités such as sweet pepper strips and carrot and celery sticks may be substituted for the pita bread.

- ¾ cup dried chick peas (6 ounces), soaked (see Note)
- ⅓ cup sesame paste (tahini)
- ¼ cup fresh lemon juice
- ¼ cup olive oil
- 2 cloves garlic, minced
- 1½ teaspoons salt
- ¼ teaspoon ground cumin
- ¼ teaspoon freshly ground pepper
- ⅓ cup chopped flat-leaf parsley
- ½ cup finely chopped black olives

  TO SERVE
- 6 pita bread pockets or 48 plain crackers
  Flat-leaf parsley sprigs

Drain chick peas in a colander. In a medium saucepan, combine peas with enough water to cover by 2 inches and bring to a boil over medium-high heat. Reduce heat to low, cover saucepan, and simmer for 1½ to 2 hours, or until chick peas are tender. Drain in the colander and let cool.

Combine chick peas, sesame paste, lemon juice, olive oil, garlic, salt, cumin, and pepper in a food processor or blender and process until smooth and slightly fluffy, about 30 to 45 seconds. Add chopped parsley and olives and process with on/off motion just until well blended.

Preheat broiler.

Split pita bread into 2 rounds and cut into fourths, then place on a baking sheet and broil until lightly toasted. Meanwhile, scoop hummus into a serving bowl and garnish with parsley sprigs. Arrange toasted pita bread on a platter around the hummus.

— MAKES 2½ CUPS HUMMUS AND 48 HORS D'OEUVRES —

Note: If using canned chick peas, use one 19-ounce can (about 2 cups) and drain well. Reduce salt to 1 teaspoon.

Sesame paste, or tahini, can also be mixed with enough water to give the consistency of heavy cream. Season it with mashed garlic, lemon juice, and salt and serve this dressing in a bowl to be spooned over a Greek mixed salad of lettuce, tomatoes, black olives, bell pepper, and Feta cheese. This makes an ideal salad to accompany barbecued meat.

THE FOURTH OF JULY

MENU

◆

*P*IMM'S

◆

*G*LAZED CHICKEN WINGS

◆

*F*RAGRANT CRUSHED OLIVES

◆

*C*APONATA PIZZAS

◆

*S*ESAME-CHEESE WAFERS

◆

*M*USSELS WITH AVOCADO SAUCE

◆

*M*INIATURE TOMATO AND MOZZARELLA KEBABS

◆

*N*ECTARINES WITH CHÈVRE, GORGONZOLA, AND PISTACHIOS

OPPOSITE: PIMM'S, MUSSELS WITH AVOCADO SAUCE, FRAGRANT CRUSHED OLIVES, CAPONATA PIZZAS, SESAME-CHEESE WAFERS

Pimm's

THIS AMBER MIXTURE WITH ITS FLAMBOYANT DECORATION IS ONE OF the most summery and pleasant English drinks. A different spirit is used in each variety of Pimm's. Pimm's No. 1 contains gin; others contain whisky, rum, or brandy.

2 cups Pimm's No. 1
4 to 6 cups chilled 7-Up or gingerale
Ice cubes

TO SERVE
4 to 6 thin slices orange, halved
8 to 12 thin slices lemon
8 to 12 thin slices cucumber
8 to 12 sprigs fresh mint
8 to 12 sprigs fresh borage

In a large pitcher, combine Pimm's and carbonated drink. Add enough ice cubes to chill mixture well.

At serving time, pour mixture into tall glasses or clear mugs. Garnish each drink with a half slice orange, a slice each of lemon and cucumber, and a sprig each of mint and borage.

— MAKES 8 TO 12 DRINKS —

Glazed Chicken Wings

PREPARE AND COOK THESE SPICY CHICKEN WINGS EARLY IN THE DAY and serve them at room temperature. Or broil them just before serving time to serve hot. Other chicken parts may also be marinated in the spicy sauce and barbecued or broiled.

4 pounds chicken wings

BARBECUE SAUCE
½ cup molasses
3 tablespoons sherry vinegar
2 tablespoons vegetable oil
1 teaspoon Worcestershire sauce

1 teaspoon coarsely ground black pepper
1 tablespoon Dijon-style mustard
½ teaspoon Tabasco
½ teaspoon salt

Cut off wing tips and halve chicken wings at joints. Arrange wing pieces in a single layer in a shallow baking dish.

In a heavy saucepan, combine molasses, vinegar, oil, Worcestershire sauce, pepper, mustard, Tabasco, and salt. Simmer over medium heat for 6 to 8 minutes, stirring occasionally. Pour sauce over the chicken pieces, cover, and refrigerate for about 3 hours, turning chicken 2 or 3 times.

About 30 minutes before cooking time, remove chicken from refrigerator and set aside to come to room temperature.

Build a medium-hot charcoal fire or preheat broiler. Arrange chicken pieces on a barbecue grill or broiler pan about 4 inches from heat and cook for 6 to 8 minutes on each side, brushing several times with remaining sauce until chicken is crisp, browned, and cooked through but still moist.

Arrange on a serving platter.

— MAKES 48 HORS D'OEUVRES —

For a spicier, less sweet glaze, marinate and baste the chicken wings with ¾ to 1 cup Crabtree & Evelyn Cabshelter Sauce.

This rich, spicy sauce was originated in the "shelters" that traditionally served meat pies, potatoes, and brown sauce to Victorian cabbies.

ℱRAGRANT CRUSHED OLIVES

THESE SEASONED OLIVES WILL BE MOST DELICIOUS IF THEY ARE PREpared a day in advance to allow the flavor to develop. To keep them for several days or longer, place olives and seasonings in a jar, add enough light vegetable oil to cover (olive oil is not necessary), and store in a cool place.

3 cups small unpitted green olives
1 tablespoon coriander seeds
1 clove garlic, thinly sliced
4 to 5 thin slices lemon, cut into six wedges each

In a mixing bowl, combine olives, coriander seed, garlic, and lemon wedges and stir to blend. Transfer mixture to a heavy clear-plastic bag and seal tightly. Place bag on a work surface so that olives are in a single layer and, using a rolling pin or wooden mallet, gently hit olives to crush them slightly without breaking bag. Place bag in the refrigerator overnight.

Transfer olives and their seasonings to an attractive dish and serve.

— MAKES 3 CUPS —

After the flavors have matured these olives can be pitted, sliced, and added to stuffings for fish or chicken or to mixed green salads.

Caponata Pizzas

THE EGGPLANT NEED NOT BE PEELED, AS THE SKIN LENDS ITS RICH color to the *caponata*. The vegetable mixture may be made up to 3 days in advance or the entire pizzas made ahead and frozen. Reheat the pizzas for about 20 minutes in a 300-degree F. oven before serving.

Caponata can also be served at room temperature on crackers, hot as an accompaniment to simple egg dishes or as a filling for an omelet, and hot or cold as a light relish with fish and meats.

To make a quicker base, make up the Currant Cream Scones on page 140, omitting the currants and sugar. When baked, split them open horizontally, spread each half with the caponata, *and broil them for 2 to 3 minutes, or until the* caponata *is heated through.*

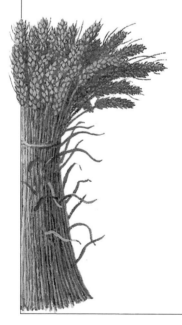

CAPONATA
3   tablespoons olive oil
½   pound eggplant (preferably very small), cut into ½-inch cubes
1   medium onion, thinly sliced
1   rib of celery, thinly sliced
1   small sweet red pepper, cored, seeded, and thinly sliced
1   clove garlic, minced
½   pound ripe tomatoes, peeled, seeded, and diced
¼   cup sliced, pitted Greek olives
1   tablespoon red-wine vinegar
    Pinch sugar
1   bay leaf
1   teaspoon chopped fresh thyme, or ¼ teaspoon dried thyme
1   tablespoon chopped fresh basil
    Salt
    Freshly ground black pepper
2   tablespoons chopped fresh parsley
1   tablespoon drained capers

PIZZA DOUGH
2¾ cups all-purpose flour
1   ¼-ounce package quick-rising dry yeast
¼   teaspoon sugar
1   teaspoon salt
¼   cup olive oil
    Cornmeal (for baking sheet)

In a large skillet, combine oil, eggplant, onion, celery, and sweet pepper and sauté over medium heat for about 4 minutes, or until softened. Add garlic and cook, stirring, about 1 minute. Stir in tomatoes, olives, vinegar, sugar, bay leaf, thyme, and basil and season with salt and pepper. Cover and simmer over low heat, stirring often, for about 20 minutes, or until vegetables are very soft. Remove cover and continue to

simmer over low heat, stirring frequently, for 15 to 20 minutes, or until most of the liquid has evaporated. Stir in parsley and capers. Taste and correct seasoning if necessary. Remove *caponata* from heat and let cool.

Meanwhile, prepare pizza dough: In a large bowl, stir together 1¾ cups of the flour, the yeast, sugar, and salt. In a saucepan, heat 1 tablespoon of the olive oil with 1 cup water until hot to the touch (105 to 115 degrees). Stir the liquid into the dry ingredients, then incorporate enough of the remaining flour to make a soft but workable dough. Knead for about 10 minutes, until the dough is smooth and elastic. Place in an oiled bowl, turning dough to coat it, cover with a damp cloth, and let rise in a warm place until double in bulk, about 30 minutes. Punch dough down and divide into 24 equal pieces.

Preheat oven to 500 degrees F.

On a lightly floured work surface, roll out each piece of dough into a thin round, about 3 inches in diameter. Sprinkle a baking sheet lightly with cornmeal and arrange 6 to 8 rounds of dough on it. Use remaining 3 tablespoons olive oil to brush the dough rounds lightly. Spread about 1 tablespoon of *caponata* evenly over each pizza, leaving a ½-inch border around the edge. Let pizzas stand for about 5 minutes before baking.

Bake in lower third of oven for 8 to 10 minutes, or until bottoms of pizzas are browned and crisp and tops are puffed and golden. Meanwhile, prepare the next baking sheet of pizzas for the oven. Continue in this manner until all are baked.

Serve warm or at room temperature.

— MAKES 24 INDIVIDUAL PIZZAS —

169

✒ESAME-CHEESE WAFERS

Cheddar and Stilton combine beautifully. The proof: mash some Stilton with an equal amount of softened unsalted butter and spread the mixture on these Cheddar wafers.

THIS SIMPLE AND VERY GOOD ACCOMPANIMENT TO DRINKS CAN BE made even more easily by omitting the second dipping of the wafers in the sesame seeds, in which case only 2 tablespoons sesame seeds are needed. The uncooked roll of dough can be frozen and thawed shortly before baking.

¼ cup sesame seeds
1 cup all-purpose flour
½ teaspoon baking powder
¼ teaspoon salt
4 tablespoons cold unsalted butter, cut into small
  pieces
¾ cup shredded sharp Cheddar cheese

Preheat oven to 350 degrees F. Spread the sesame seeds over a baking sheet and toast for about 10 minutes, or until they are lightly colored and fragrant. Remove from the oven and set aside to cool.

Combine flour, baking powder, and salt in a food processor and pulse to blend. Add butter and cheese and process until mixture resembles coarse crumbs. Add 2 tablespoons cold water and process until mixture forms a ball, adding ½ tablespoon more water if necessary to make dough hold together.

Shape dough into a log about 1½ inches in diameter. Spread the toasted sesame seeds on a sheet of waxed paper and roll the log in the sesame seeds until the surface is covered. Wrap log in plastic wrap and chill for at least 2 hours or overnight. Place remaining sesame seeds in a small dish.

Preheat the oven to 425 degrees F.

With a sharp knife, cut dough log into ⅛-inch-thick slices. Dip one side of each wafer in the remaining sesame seeds to cover and place wafers, seeded-sides-up and spaced slightly apart, on ungreased baking sheets. Bake wafers for 7 to 10 minutes, or until nicely golden and let cool on wire racks.

— MAKES ABOUT 48 WAFERS —

Mussels with Avocado Sauce

THE AVOCADO SAUCE IS ALSO SUPERB ON SLICED TOMATOES OR OVER A platter of fresh shrimp.

3 pounds mussels (about 4 dozen)
½ cup dry white wine
1 teaspoon minced shallot
1 bay leaf

SAUCE
1 medium ripe avocado
1 tablespoon fresh lemon juice
1 small fresh jalapeño pepper, cored, seeded, and chopped
½ small sweet green pepper, cored, seeded, and chopped
4 tablespoons sliced green onion (white with some green)
1 tablespoon chopped fresh cilantro leaves
1 clove garlic, minced
⅛ teaspoon ground cumin
Salt
Freshly ground black pepper

TO SERVE
48 small fresh cilantro leaves
Lemon wedges

Thoroughly scrub mussel shells and remove beards. In a large saucepan, combine mussels with the wine, shallot, bay leaf, and ½ cup water. Cover, bring liquid to a boil, and steam mussels over medium-low heat for 4 to 5 minutes, or until mussels open. Remove from heat and let cool slightly, discarding any mussels that did not open. Remove mussels from their shells, tearing off and discarding half of each shell and placing other half in a colander. Rinse shells thoroughly to remove grit, pat them dry, and return mussels to cleaned half shells. Arrange in a spiral or concentric circles pattern on a large round serving platter.

In a small bowl mash avocado with lemon juice, then beat to a smooth purée. Stir in jalapeño pepper, green pepper, green onion, chopped cilantro, garlic, and cumin, season with salt and pepper, and stir until well blended.

Spoon about 1 teaspoon avocado sauce over each mussel. Garnish with a cilantro leaf, place lemon wedges in center of the platter, and serve.

— MAKES ABOUT 48 HORS D'OEUVRES —

*M*INIATURE TOMATO AND MOZZARELLA KEBABS

The main ingredients here can be the makings of a summery salad in the colors of the Italian flag. Slice the mozzarella ¼ inch thick and the tomatoes ½ inch thick. Arrange them, alternating and overlapping them, with basil sprigs on a serving dish and dress the salad simply with a mixture of 1 tablespoon sherry vinegar, 3 to 5 tablespoons olive oil, and salt and pepper to taste.

THE SKEWERS OF CHEESE AND TOMATO MAY BE ASSEMBLED SEVERAL hours ahead, wrapped tightly, and refrigerated. Bring to room temperature before dressing and serving.

- 8 ounces mozzarella cheese, cut into ½-inch cubes
- 3 to 4 unpeeled ripe tomatoes, seeded and cut into ¾-inch cubes
- 1 large bunch fresh basil (see Note)
- 3 tablespoons olive oil
- 2 teaspoons red-wine vinegar
- ½ teaspoon Dijon-style mustard
  Salt
  Freshly ground pepper

Thread 1 cube of cheese and 1 cube of tomato onto each of 45 wooden toothpicks.

Shred enough of the fresh basil leaves to make about 2 tablespoons and set aside. Use some of the remaining basil leaves to line a serving platter. Arrange cheese and tomato skewers on the bed of basil.

In a small bowl, whisk together oil, vinegar, and mustard until emulsified.

Just before serving, drizzle vinaigrette evenly over skewers, sprinkle shredded basil over cheese and tomato skewers, and season lightly with salt and freshly ground pepper.

— MAKES 45 HORS D'OEUVRES —

Note: If fresh basil is not available, replace the 2 tablespoons fresh with 2 teaspoons dried and line the platter with fresh parsley.

Nectarines with Chèvre, Gorgonzola, and Pistachios

THIS IS A DO-IT-YOURSELF HORS D'OEUVRE FOR AN INFORMAL SUMMER cocktail party. If the blended cheeses seem a bit too thick to spread easily, thin them with a teaspoon or so of cream or milk.

3 ounces Montrachet cheese or other soft chèvre,
   softened
1½ ounces Gorgonzola cheese, softened
4 ripe nectarines
   Fresh lemon juice
¼ cup chopped pistachios

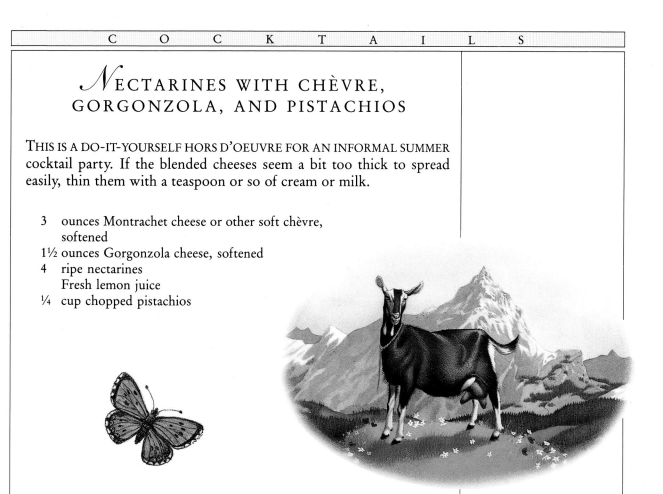

Combine Montrachet and Gorgonzola in a small bowl and beat until thoroughly blended and smooth.

Cut 1 nectarine in half, remove pit, and cut each half into 2 or 3 bite-size wedges. Brush cut sides of fruit lightly with lemon juice. Spread a little of the cheese mixture in the indentation of each nectarine wedge. Then top each wedge with chopped pistachios to coat cheese lightly.

Transfer remaining cheese mixture to a small glass serving bowl. Place remaining pistachios in a small shallow serving bowl. Arrange the prepared fruit wedges, the 3 remaining uncut nectarines, and the bowls of cheese and pistachios on a large serving platter or wooden board, along with small knives for cutting the fruit and spreading the cheese. The prepared fruit wedges will serve as examples, showing guests how to slice, spread, and top the remaining nectarines themselves. (Remaining nectarines need not be brushed with lemon juice.)

— MAKES 16 TO 24 HORS D'OEUVRES —

PUTTING ON THE RITZ

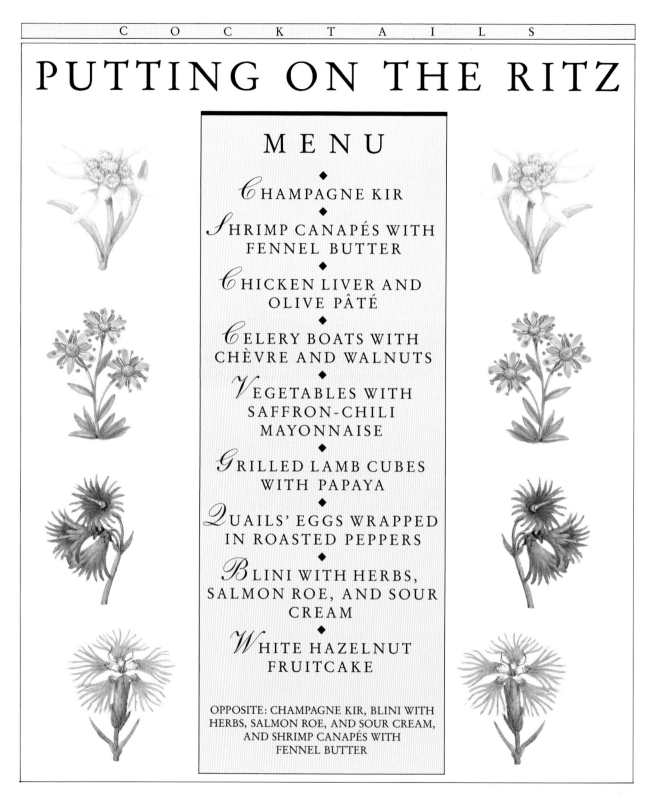

MENU

◆

*C*HAMPAGNE KIR

◆

*S*HRIMP CANAPÉS WITH
FENNEL BUTTER

◆

*C*HICKEN LIVER AND
OLIVE PÂTÉ

◆

*C*ELERY BOATS WITH
CHÈVRE AND WALNUTS

◆

*V*EGETABLES WITH
SAFFRON-CHILI
MAYONNAISE

◆

*G*RILLED LAMB CUBES
WITH PAPAYA

◆

*Q*UAILS' EGGS WRAPPED
IN ROASTED PEPPERS

◆

*B*LINI WITH HERBS,
SALMON ROE, AND SOUR
CREAM

◆

*W*HITE HAZELNUT
FRUITCAKE

OPPOSITE: CHAMPAGNE KIR, BLINI WITH
HERBS, SALMON ROE, AND SOUR CREAM,
AND SHRIMP CANAPÉS WITH
FENNEL BUTTER

CHAMPAGNE KIR

SPARKLING AND FESTIVE, THIS IS A VARIATION ON THE CLASSIC KIR made with white Burgundy and cassis. Measure the black currant liqueur into glasses in advance and pour the Champagne in at the last moment: It will blend with the cassis with no stirring necessary.

    2   bottles Champagne, chilled
    ½   cup cassis or black currant syrup
    12 to 14 thin curls of lemon zest (optional)

Pour 2 teaspoons cassis into each Champagne flute. Fill glasses three-quarters full with Champagne. Drop a curl of lemon zest into each glass.

— MAKES 12 TO 14 DRINKS —

SHRIMP CANAPÉS WITH FENNEL BUTTER

THE CANAPÉS MAY BE ASSEMBLED 2 TO 3 HOURS AHEAD, BUT THE fennel sprigs should be added just before serving. Prepare the fennel butter at least 1 day ahead—or as many as 3 days—so that the flavors develop. Its light texture and delicate taste make it an excellent seasoning for vegetables and fish. To have a supply on hand, shape the butter into a log, wrap and refrigerate it until set, slice into ¼-inch-thick pats (keeping the log shape), then rewrap well and freeze. Thaw and use the individual pats as needed.

    1½ pounds fresh medium shrimp (about 50) in their
        shells

    FENNEL MARINADE
    ½   cup light olive oil
    2   tablespoons white-wine vinegar
    1   tablespoon fresh lemon juice
    2   teaspoons Pernod or other anise-flavored liqueur
    2   teaspoons Dijon-style mustard
    1   clove garlic, halved
    ¾   teaspoon salt
    ¼   teaspoon crushed fennel seed
    ⅛   teaspoon freshly ground pepper

FENNEL BUTTER

⅔ cup fennel leaves
3 tablespoons fresh parsley leaves
1 cup (2 sticks) unsalted butter, softened
1 tablespoon fresh lemon juice
1 tablespoon Pernod or other anise-flavored liqueur
¾ teaspoon salt
⅛ teaspoon ground cayenne
¾ cup finely minced fennel bulb

TO ASSEMBLE

25 thin slices firm white sandwich bread
Fennel sprigs

Bring a large saucepan of lightly salted water to a boil, add shrimp, and boil for about 2 minutes, or until they turn pink. Turn shrimp into a colander, refresh under cold water to stop cooking, and drain. Remove shells and use a small knife to remove black veins from shrimp. Carefully slice each shrimp in half lengthwise and set aside in a shallow glass or other non-reactive dish.

In a small bowl, stir together oil, vinegar, lemon juice, Pernod, mustard, garlic, salt, fennel seed, and pepper until well blended. Pour marinade over shrimp and chill in the refrigerator for at least 2 hours or up to 8 hours, turning once or twice.

To prepare fennel butter, finely chop fennel and parsley leaves in a food processor, add butter, and process until well combined. With the motor running, add lemon juice and Pernod through the feed tube. Season with salt and cayenne and stir in minced fennel bulb.

To assemble, remove shrimp from the marinade and pat dry on paper towels. Spread each bread slice with fennel butter (butter should be room temperature). Using a 1½-inch round biscuit cutter, cut 4 rounds from each bread slice or cut bread into 4 squares. Place a shrimp half, pink side up, on each canapé, cover loosely with plastic wrap, and chill in the refrigerator for at least 20 minutes to firm butter. To serve, garnish each canapé with a fennel sprig and arrange on a serving platter.

— MAKES 100 HORS D'OEUVRES —

The French canon, Félix Kir, eminent cleric, mayor of Dijon, and distinguished member of the French Resistance during World War II, may be longest remembered for inventing the cooling apéritif that bears his name.

*C*HICKEN LIVER AND OLIVE PÂTÉ

THIS PÂTÉ CAN ALSO BE SERVED AS A FIRST COURSE AT DINNER ON buttered toast, in which case it looks particularly appetizing brought to the table in a pâté dish and covered with a thin layer of clarified butter and a sprinkling of thyme.

¾ pound chicken livers
2 tablespoons Madeira or medium sherry
2 tablespoons milk
½ cup (1 stick) unsalted butter
½ cup chopped onion
2 tablespoons Cognac or other brandy
½ teaspoon salt
⅛ teaspoon freshly ground pepper
⅛ teaspoon ground mace
¼ cup pitted and slivered black olives, preferably Kalamata or Niçoise
1 box (7 ounces) Crabtree & Evelyn Cream Crackers or other cream crackers

To make clarified butter, in a small saucepan melt ½ pound (2 sticks) butter over low heat, remove it from the heat, and let it stand for several minutes, or until the milky residue sinks to the bottom. Then pour the clear yellow butter into another container, taking care that none of the residue mixes with it. This butter keeps for weeks in the refrigerator and is also an excellent frying and sautéeing medium, as it burns less easily than unclarified butter.

Trim tough membranes and any yellow patches from chicken livers and separate each into 2 lobes. Let soak in a small bowl with Madeira and milk for at least 3 hours or overnight.

In a large skillet, melt 1 tablespoon of the butter, add onions, and cook, stirring occasionally, over medium heat for 5 minutes, or until softened and lightly browned. Spoon onions into a food processor and set skillet aside.

Pour off and discard soaking liquid from chicken livers and pat the livers dry on paper towels. Melt 2 tablespoons of the remaining butter in skillet in which onions were browned. When butter is hot, add chicken livers and sauté, stirring occasionally, over medium-high heat for about 5 minutes, or until browned and firm but still pale pink inside. Using a slotted spoon, transfer chicken livers to the food processor.

Remove skillet from heat and add Cognac. Return skillet to the stove, increase heat to high, and cook, stirring to scrap up brown bits, for 3 minutes. Add pan juices to food processor.

Cut remaining 5 tablespoons butter into several pieces. Start processing chicken liver mixture, adding butter one piece at a time through feed tube until mixture is a smooth purée. Add salt, pepper, and mace and continue to process until thoroughly blended and smooth. Transfer mixture to a bowl and stir in slivered olives. Taste and correct seasoning, if necessary. Pack the pâté into a crock, cover tightly, and place in the refrigerator to chill for at least 4 hours or up to 2 to 3 days to allow flavors to develop and blend.

Remove pâté from refrigerator 1 hour before serving. Serve with cream crackers.

— MAKES ABOUT 30 HORS D'OEUVRES —

Celery Boats with Chèvre and Walnuts

CELERY, CHEESE, AND BUTTER, ACCOMPANIED BY CRACKERS AND A bowl of nuts, is a traditional ending to many English lunches and dinners. This hors d'oeuvre includes the best flavors and textures of that combination. It can be prepared several hours in advance, covered with plastic wrap, and refrigerated until half an hour before serving.

6 to 8 large celery stalks
8 ounces chèvre, softened
½ cup (1 stick) unsalted butter, softened
40 walnut halves

TO SERVE
Celery or fresh parsley leaves

Trim celery stalks, remove strings, rinse, and pat dry. Trim off a thin lengthwise strip along the rounded back of each stalk to form a flat bottom.

Trim off and discard rind from the chèvre, if necessary, and blend cheese with butter in a food processor with an on/off motion until smooth.

Spoon cheese mixture into the hollows of celery, mounding it nicely, and top with walnut halves, spaced ½ inch apart along the length of the celery. Using a sharp knife, cut on a sharp diagonal between walnuts to form bite-size pieces. Arrange on a serving platter and top each piece with a celery or parsley leaf.

— MAKES ABOUT 40 HORS D'OEUVRES —

VEGETABLES WITH SAFFRON-CHILI MAYONNAISE

A lemony bagna cauda— *or garlic and anchovy "hot bath"—is a tempting optional sauce for these vegetables. In a small heavy saucepan, gently heat ½ cup olive oil with 2 tablespoons unsalted butter. Stir in 2 tablespoons lemon juice, 5 mashed anchovy fillets, and 3 crushed garlic cloves. Simmer gently for 5 minutes. Pour the sauce (minus the garlic cloves) into a small pot or heatproof bowl set over a candle warmer. Put pot and warmer in the center of a heatproof tray or wooden board and arrange the vegetables around it. Guests choose a vegetable "dipper" and swirl it in the sauce to keep the mixture well blended as it coats the vegetables.*

CHOOSE A SELECTION OF BABY VEGETABLES AND/OR OTHERS THAT can be served whole or cut into bite-size pieces. The blanched vegetables are equally delicious warm or cold, arranged in Chinese steamer baskets or on any shallow basket or platter.

SAFFRON-CHILI MAYONNAISE
3 tablespoons white-wine vinegar
12 saffron threads (approximately)
2 large egg yolks
1 small fresh hot red chili pepper, cored and seeded, or ¼ to ½ teaspoon ground cayenne (see Note)
1 small clove garlic
¾ teaspoon salt
1½ cups olive oil
 Pinch sugar

1½ pounds fresh baby vegetables or small, individual vegetables suitable for dipping such as beets, carrots, squash, snow peas, sugar snap peas, green beans, asparagus spears, broccoli, cauliflower, and new potatoes

TO SERVE
Salt
Freshly ground black pepper
Paprika

In a small saucepan, warm vinegar and 1 tablespoon water briefly over low heat, add crumbled saffron threads, and remove pan from heat. Let saffron steep for 10 minutes.

In a food processor or a mixing bowl, process or whisk briefly egg yolks, saffron mixture, chili pepper, garlic, and salt just until blended. Through feed tube or whisking vigorously by hand, add oil, a tablespoon at a time, until the mixture begins to thicken. Add remaining oil in a thin, steady stream, processing or whisking continuously until oil is thoroughly incorporated and mixture is quite thick and smooth. Add sugar, taste, and add more salt if necessary and blend.

To prepare vegetables, rinse and drain, leaving on some of stems of carrots, squash, and beets. Remove strings from snow peas, sugar snap

peas, and green beans. Trim asparagus spears. Trim broccoli and cauliflower into flowerets.

Bring to a boil a large pot of lightly salted water. Blanch vegetables separately or in logical groupings (snow peas, sugar snaps, green beans, and asparagus together; carrots and squash together; broccoli and cauliflower together, etc.) until just crisp-tender. Cooking times will vary: Peas, beans, and asparagus will need only 30 seconds; most others will require 1 to 2 minutes; new potatoes should cook for 5 to 8 minutes. Plunge vegetables as they are blanched into cold water to stop cooking and to set color, then drain and pat dry thoroughly with paper towels. If not serving immediately, wrap vegetables in plastic wrap and refrigerate.

To serve, arrange vegetables in Chinese steamer baskets or any other basket or serving platter and sprinkle lightly with salt and pepper. Transfer saffron-chili mayonnaise to a small serving bowl, sprinkle lightly with paprika, and serve with the blanched vegetables for dipping. If desired, vegetables can be steam-warmed over gently boiling water in a wok before serving.

— MAKES 30 TO 40 HORS D'OEUVRES (1¾ CUPS MAYONNAISE) —

Note: If chili pepper or cayenne is unavailable, replace ¼ to ½ cup of the olive oil in the recipe with an equal amount of Crabtree & Evelyn's fiery Olive and Sunflower Oil with Herbs.

GRILLED LAMB CUBES WITH PAPAYA

THE SKEWERS OF LAMB AND PAPAYA CAN BE ASSEMBLED UP TO 4 HOURS before cooking.

1 pound boneless leg of lamb or shoulder, cut into 1-inch cubes

MARINADE
⅓ cup olive oil
2 tablespoons red-wine vinegar
1 clove garlic, chopped
¾ teaspoon ground cumin
½ teaspoon ground cayenne
½ teaspoon salt
½ teaspoon freshly ground black pepper
¼ teaspoon ground coriander seed

TO ASSEMBLE
2 ripe but firm papayas, peeled, seeded, and cut into ¾-inch cubes
2 tablespoons fresh lemon juice
30 wooden skewers (6 inches long)

Papayas are often picked—and sold— green. Ripen them in a warm, sunny spot until they become more yellow than green and have begun to soften.

Place lamb cubes in a shallow glass or non-reactive dish.

In a small bowl, whisk together oil, vinegar, garlic, cumin, cayenne, salt, black pepper, and coriander seed. Pour marinade over lamb, stirring gently to coat meat well. Set aside at room temperature and let marinate for 2 hours; or chill in the refrigerator for up to 8 hours.

Place skewers in a shallow dish, add enough water to cover, and let soak for at least 1 hour before assembling and cooking lamb and papaya.

Build a charcoal fire on a grill or preheat broiler.

Meanwhile, in a mixing bowl sprinkle papaya cubes with lemon juice and toss gently to coat fruit thoroughly.

Drain skewers. Then thread cubes of marinated lamb and papaya onto each skewer. Brush each lightly with remaining marinade.

When coals have burned down to a moderately hot fire, arrange skewers around edge so that blunt ends are not directly over coals. Grill for 5 to 10 minutes, brushing with marinade and using blunt ends of skewers as handles for turning meat occasionally so that all sides brown equally. Lamb should be nicely browned all over but still pink inside. Arrange attractively on a platter and serve immediately.

— MAKES 30 HORS D'OEUVRES —

$\mathcal{Q}$UAILS' EGGS WRAPPED IN ROASTED PEPPERS

USING GREEN, YELLOW, AND RED SWEET PEPPERS MAKES THIS A PARticularly colorful presentation when served on a plain white plate. Wrap the eggs in pepper strips several hours in advance, cover lightly, and refrigerate. Remove from the refrigerator long enough in advance to warm to room temperature. Then dip eggs in the oil and herbs just before serving.

24 quails' eggs
1 each green, red, and yellow sweet peppers
¼ cup finely minced mixed fresh herbs such as parsley, chives, thyme, chervil, dill, and marjoram
1 teaspoon salt
2 tablespoons olive or hazelnut oil
24 toothpicks

Put any extra strips of roasted bell pepper into a jar and cover them with olive oil. These can be refrigerated for up to 2 weeks and served in salads and rice dishes or with grilled meats. The resulting oil contributes an elusive and delicious flavor to vinaigrettes.

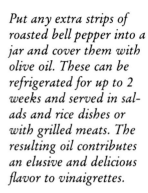

Place eggs in a saucepan. Add enough hot water to cover them by about 2 inches, bring to a boil, and boil for 2 minutes. Drain off water and refresh eggs under cold water to stop the cooking. Let cool completely.

Meanwhile, roast the peppers. Pierce the stem end of each pepper with a wooden-handled kitchen fork and hold pepper directly over gas burner, turning slowly, until all sides are well charred. Or place peppers on a baking sheet and broil under preheated broiler as close to heat source as possible, turning occasionally, until thoroughly charred. Place peppers in a paper bag and close it tightly to allow peppers to steam for several minutes. Remove from the bag and rinse peppers under cold water, rubbing off blackened skin with the fingers. Halve each pepper lengthwise and remove core, seeds, and membrane. Cut each lengthwise into ½-inch-wide strips.

Peel the eggs, cracking the shell all over and starting to peel at the blunt end, where there is usually an air pocket that makes the peeling easier. Wrap each egg in a strip of roasted pepper and secure in place with a toothpick.

In a small dish, combine herbs and salt and mix well. In another dish, place the oil. Dip half of each pepper-wrapped egg into the oil, then dip in the herb mixture. Arrange on a platter and serve.

— MAKES 24 HORS D'OEUVRES —

WHITE HAZELNUT FRUITCAKE

AS THIS CAKE HAS A PARTICULARLY FINE TEXTURE AND FLAVOR AND keeps well, it is a very good one to have on hand during holiday seasons. The cake needs 3 days to mellow, but it can be made 2 weeks ahead and moistened by sprinkling the cheesecloth with a few spoonfuls of rum.

1 cup coarsely chopped dried apricots
½ cup coarsely chopped dried pears
½ cup coarsely chopped dried figs
½ cup coarsely chopped dried pineapple
1 cup golden raisins
½ cup chopped citron
1 cup dark rum
2 cups whole hazelnuts
3⅔ cups all-purpose flour
2 teaspoons baking powder
1 teaspoon salt
1½ cups (3 sticks) unsalted butter, softened
2½ cups sugar
7 large eggs, separated
2 teaspoons freshly grated lemon zest
1 teaspoon freshly grated nutmeg
2 teaspoons orange flower water
1 teaspoon vanilla extract

In a mixing bowl, combine apricots, pears, figs, pineapple, golden raisins, and citron with ⅔ cup of the rum and set fruit aside to macerate for several hours or overnight.

Preheat oven to 350 degrees F.

Spread hazelnuts in a single layer on a baking sheet. Bake in center of hot oven, stirring frequently and watching carefully, for 6 to 8 minutes, or until nuts are toasted and fragrant. Remove nuts from oven, wrap immediately in a clean dish cloth, and rub vigorously on a work surface to remove skins. Discard skins and chop nuts coarsely. (If the hazelnuts are already skinned, simply roast them for 6 to 8 minutes and coarsely chop.) Add to macerating fruit.

Reduce oven temperature to 325 degrees F.

Sift flour with baking powder and salt onto a sheet of waxed paper and set aside.

In a large mixing bowl, cream together butter and sugar and beat in the egg yolks, one at a time, beating for about 1 minute after each addition, until mixture becomes very light and fluffy. Add lemon zest, nutmeg, flower water, vanilla, and flour mixture and beat until well blended. Stir in fruit, hazelnuts, and macerating liquid.

In a very clean large bowl, beat egg whites until stiff but not dry peaks form. Stir about one-fourth of whites into fruitcake batter to lighten, then gently fold in remaining whites. (The batter will be heavy, so it may be easiest to fold whites in with your hands.)

Spoon batter into a 10-inch tube pan that has been buttered, lined with buttered parchment paper, and floured. Smooth top of batter with a spatula. Bake in center of oven for 1 hour and 10 minutes to 1 hour and 20 minutes, or until cake is a rich golden brown and a toothpick inserted into center comes out clean.

Remove from oven and let cool in pan for 15 minutes. Using a small knife, loosen edges of cake and turn out onto a wire rack to cool completely.

In a bowl, soak in remaining ⅓ cup rum a square of cheesecloth large enough to completely wrap cake. Spread the rum-soaked cheesecloth on a large sheet of aluminum foil. Place cake in center and wrap tightly with the cheesecloth and then with the foil. Put in a cool dry place to mellow for at least 3 days. To serve, remove from the wrappings and slice very thinly.

— MAKES ABOUT 24 THIN SLICES —

The unusual combination of fruits and nuts gives this cake its distinctive taste. Other dried and candied citrus fruits and peels may be used—as well as almonds or walnuts—in your favorite combination, as long as the total quantity is the same as in the recipe.

*B*LINI WITH HERBS, SALMON ROE, AND SOUR CREAM

BLINI ARE BEST FRESH, PREPARED JUST BEFORE ASSEMBLING AND SERV-ing. But they can also be made in advance, arranged in a single layer on a baking sheet, and covered loosely with foil. Reheat for 10 minutes in a 325-degree F. oven just before topping with sour cream and salmon roe. They are particularly attractive when served on a silver platter lined with a starched white linen napkin.

BLINI
¾ cup milk
3 tablespoons unsalted butter
1¼ cups all-purpose flour
1½ teaspoons quick-rising dry yeast
1 teaspoon sugar
½ teaspoon salt
2 large eggs, separated
2 tablespoons minced fresh chives
2 tablespoons minced fresh parsley

TO ASSEMBLE
½ cup sour cream or *crème fraîche*
½ cup red salmon roe
 Freshly ground pepper
35 flat-leaf parsley leaves
 Butter for cooking blini

In a small saucepan, heat milk and butter over low heat until butter is almost melted, remove from the heat, and set aside to allow butter to finish melting and liquid to cool to lukewarm.

Meanwhile, combine flour, yeast, sugar, and salt in a food processor and pulse with on/off motion to blend. With motor running pour milk mixture through feed tube into dry ingredients and pulse to blend. Add egg yolks and pulse until well mixed. Transfer batter into a mixing bowl, cover, and set aside in a warm place to rise for about 40 minutes, or until double in bulk.

Heat a griddle or large, heavy frying pan until hot. Beat egg whites until stiff and fold them, along with chives and parsley, into the risen batter.

Butter hot griddle just enough to prevent the blini from sticking. Drop batter by ½ tablespoons onto griddle, spreading it out if necessary to make 1½-inch rounds. Cook each side for about 40 seconds, adjusting heat if necessary so that blini brown nicely without burning.

To assemble, spread ¾ teaspoon sour cream over the top of each blini. Top with ¾ teaspoon salmon roe and grind a little pepper over the top. Garnish each with a parsley leaf.

— MAKES 35 HORS D'OEUVRES —

These are often made in part or entirely with buckwheat flour; the result is less light but more flavorful. Thin slivers of pickled herring or smoked salmon, trout, or bluefish can be substituted for the salmon roe.

DINNER

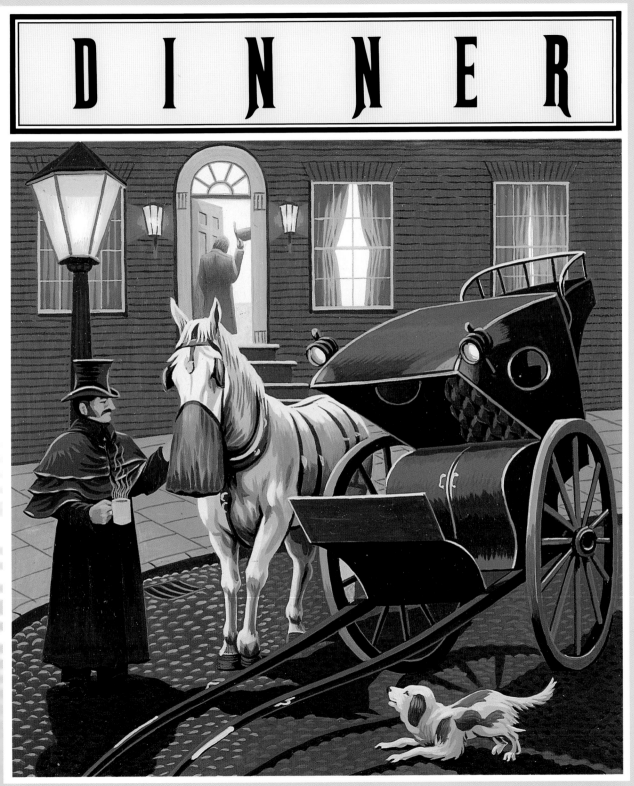

MIDSUMMER'S NIGHT

M E N U

◆

*M*ELON AND
PROSCIUTTO SALAD
WITH LIME-PEPPER
VINAIGRETTE

◆

*M*ARINATED TUNA
STEAKS WITH TOMATO-
BASIL SAUCE

◆

*B*ABY SQUASH WITH
NASTURTIUM BUTTER

◆

*L*EMON RICE

◆

*P*EACH LATTICE PIE

PHOTO: MARINATED SWORDFISH STEAK
WITH TOMATO-BASIL SAUCE

MELON AND PROSCIUTTO SALAD WITH LIME-PEPPER VINAIGRETTE

ANY COMBINATION OF THREE RIPE MELONS CAN BE USED, BUT A mixture of colors produces the prettiest salad.

½ fresh cantaloupe
½ fresh honeydew melon
½ fresh Cranshaw melon

LIME-PEPPER VINAIGRETTE
¼ cup fresh lime juice
2 teaspoons honey
1 teaspoon Crabtree & Evelyn Provençal Herbs
   Mustard or Dijon-style mustard
½ teaspoon coarsely ground pepper
¼ teaspoon grated lime zest
¼ cup walnut oil
¼ cup safflower or sunflower oil
   Salt

TO ASSEMBLE
2 medium bunches watercress
6 thin slices prosciutto or Westphalian ham

Scoop out and discard seeds from melon halves and slice each half into neat ¼- to ½-inch-thick slices. Trim off rind and discard.

In a mixing bowl, whisk together lime juice, honey, mustard, pepper, and lime zest. Slowly add walnut oil and safflower oil, whisking until dressing is thoroughly blended. Season to taste with salt, according to saltiness of ham.

Snap off and discard tough stems from watercress, add leaves to dressing, and toss to coat lightly.

Divide watercress salad among 6 large salad plates, arrange slightly overlapping slices of cantaloupe, honeydew, and Cranshaw in center, and drape a slice of prosciutto over each serving. Serve immediately.

— 6 SERVINGS —

These ingredients also make wonderful summer hors d'oeuvres. Cut the melon into finger-size sticks, lay a sprig of watercress on each, and wrap in a slice of prosciutto so that the watercress leaves stick out from one end. Build into triangular piles on a serving platter, with the leafy ends alternately facing front and back.

ℬABY SQUASH
WITH NASTURTIUM BUTTER

IF BABY SQUASH IS NOT AVAILABLE, USE THICKLY SLICED SMALL ZUC-chini and summer squash.

  1½ pounds assorted baby squash such as zucchini,
       summer squash, pattypan, and butternut
  6 tablespoons unsalted butter
  2 teaspoons finely chopped shallot
  3 tablespoons unsprayed fresh nasturtium leaves,
       rinsed, patted dry, and chopped
  3 tablespoons unsprayed fresh nasturtium blossoms,
       rinsed, patted dry, and chopped
  1 teaspoon shallot-flavored white-wine vinegar
      Salt
      Freshly ground pepper

      TO SERVE
      Whole unsprayed fresh nasturtium blossoms and
      leaves

The peppery taste of nasturtium leaves lends itself to flavoring vegetables and salads, while the leaves between thin slices of lightly buttered bread make delicate tea sandwiches.

Place squash in a steamer basket set in a large saucepan of 1½ to 2 inches boiling water and steam it for 3 to 6 minutes, or until just tender. (Steaming time will vary with size of squash.)

Meanwhile, melt butter in a medium skillet, add shallot, and sauté until softened, about 3 minutes. Stir in chopped nasturtium leaves and blossoms and vinegar and simmer over low heat, stirring, for about 1 minute. Season with salt and pepper. (Nasturtiums have a peppery taste, so add pepper sparingly.)

Add warm steamed squash to skillet and toss gently to coat well with nasturtium butter. To serve, place on a large platter and garnish with whole nasturtium blossoms and leaves.

— 6 SERVINGS —

191

MARINATED TUNA STEAKS WITH TOMATO-BASIL SAUCE

IF FRESH TUNA IS NOT AVAILABLE, SWORDFISH CAN BE SUBSTITUTED, IN which case the cooking time should be increased to 5 to 6 minutes per side, because swordfish is not usually served medium-rare. The sauce can be made a few hours in advance and reheated just before serving.

6   fresh 1-inch-thick tuna steaks (about 6 ounces each)
    Coarsely ground pepper
6   tablespoons olive oil
2   tablespoons fresh lemon juice
2   tablespoons chopped fresh oregano, or 2 teaspoons dried

TOMATO-BASIL SAUCE
1½ tablespoons unsalted butter
1½ tablespoons olive oil
3   tablespoons finely chopped shallot
2   tablespoons red wine
1   tablespoon sherry vinegar
1   pound plum tomatoes, peeled, seeded, and diced
1½ tablespoons shredded fresh basil leaves
    Salt
    Freshly ground pepper

TO SERVE
6   small sprigs fresh oregano
6   small fresh basil leaves

The tomato-basil sauce can double as a lovely fresh summer pasta sauce, particularly when paired with mushroom tortellini.

Sprinkle tuna steaks on both sides with pepper.

Combine oil, lemon juice, and chopped oregano in a shallow glass or non-reactive dish just large enough to hold tuna steaks in a single layer and stir to blend. Add tuna steaks, turning them to coat both sides with marinade. Set aside at room temperature and let marinate for 1 hour, turning once or twice.

Build a charcoal fire in a grill or preheat broiler.

Meanwhile, in a medium skillet melt butter with oil over medium heat, add shallot, and cook until softened, about 3 minutes. Add wine and vinegar and reduce over high heat, stirring, for about 1 minute. Reduce heat to medium-low, add tomatoes, and simmer for 5 to 6 minutes, or until most of the liquid is evaporated. Stir in shredded basil, season with salt and pepper, and simmer for 30 seconds. Keep warm while grilling tuna.

When coals have burned down to medium-hot or when broiler is heated, place tuna steaks on grill or broiler tray 4 to 5 inches from fire and cook each side for about 4 minutes, or until tuna is medium-rare in center. Season with salt, if desired.

Place tuna steaks on a large platter, spoon tomato-basil sauce over top, and garnish each steak with a sprig of oregano and a basil leaf. Serve immediately.

— 6 SERVINGS —

*L*EMON RICE

ALTHOUGH THIS RESTS OFF THE HEAT FOR SEVERAL MINUTES BEFORE being served, it will stay hot if a heavy saucepan is used.

4 tablespoons butter
¾ cup chopped celery with some leaves
⅓ cup chopped green onion (whites and some green)
1½ cups uncooked white rice
2¼ cups chicken stock
1½ tablespoons fresh lemon juice
1 tablespoon grated fresh lemon zest
1 teaspoon salt (see Note)
⅛ teaspoon freshly ground pepper
1 small bay leaf

TO SERVE
¼ cup minced fresh parsley

In a heavy 2-quart saucepan, melt butter over medium-low heat. Add celery and green onion and cook until softened, about 5 minutes. Stir in rice and cook, stirring, for 1 to 2 minutes, coating all grains with the butter. Stir in stock, lemon juice, lemon zest, salt, pepper, and bay leaf. Bring to a boil, reduce heat to low, cover pan, and simmer for 20 to 25 minutes, or until all liquid is absorbed and rice is tender. Remove from heat and let stand, covered, for 5 to 8 minutes.

Discard bay leaf. Add parsley and toss rice lightly with a fork to mix and fluff. Serve hot.

— 6 SERVINGS —

Note: If using canned chicken broth instead of homemade stock, reduce quantity of salt to ½ teaspoon or less.

Lemon and rice combine well in sweet dishes, too. For an old-fashioned rice pudding with a light, delicate flavor, combine ⅓ cup raw rice with ¼ cup sugar, three 2-inch strips of lemon zest, and 2½ cups milk in a 1-quart overproof dish and bake the mixture in a 300 degree F. oven for about 1½ hours, stirring every half hour. Serve with heavy whipped cream.

$\mathcal{P}$EACH LATTICE PIE

THIS PASTRY DOUGH CAN BE MADE A DAY IN ADVANCE AND REFRIGERATED. Or prepare the dough up to a week in advance and freeze it. If the dough is too firm to roll, let it stand at room temperature for several minutes until it is just warm enough to work with. If desired, serve the pie with vanilla ice cream flavored with a little ground cinnamon.

PASTRY DOUGH
2   cups plus 2 tablespoons all-purpose flour
1   teaspoon sugar
1   teaspoon salt
7   tablespoons cold unsalted butter
6   tablespoons cold lard or solid vegetable shortening
1   large egg yolk
1½ teaspoons white-wine vinegar

PEACH FILLING
¾   to 1 cup sugar (according to sweetness of fruit)
3   tablespoons cornstarch
¼   teaspoon ground mace
¼   teaspoon salt
3   pounds fresh peaches, peeled and thickly sliced
    (about 7 cups)
1   tablespoon fresh lemon juice
1   tablespoon dry sherry

TO ASSEMBLE
2   tablespoons peach or apricot preserves
1   tablespoon heavy cream
2   teaspoons sugar

To prepare pastry dough, combine flour, sugar, and salt in a large mixing bowl. Add butter and lard and work it into flour mixture with your fingers or a fork until mixture resembles small peas.

In a small bowl, whisk together egg yolk, vinegar, and 3 tablespoons cold water until well blended. Sprinkle liquid over flour mixture and toss with a fork just until ingredients are moistened and can be formed into a ball. If mixture seems too dry, add up to 1 tablespoon more cold water by teaspoonsful, until a dough forms. Divide dough into two balls, one somewhat larger than the other, flatten balls slightly, and wrap each in plastic wrap. Chill in the refrigerator for at least 30 minutes.

Crabtree & Evelyn flower waters and "fruit only" conserves can provide variations for this pie. Give the peaches a light, slightly floral taste and aroma by substituting 1 tablespoon orange flower water or rose-water for the sherry in the filling. These natural extracts from the distillation of orange and rose blossoms were an important ingredient in British cooking from Elizabethan times until the nineteenth century and are now enjoying a deserved revival in modern cooking.

Meanwhile, in a large mixing bowl combine sugar, cornstarch, mace, and salt. Add peaches, lemon juice, and sherry and toss gently to coat peaches well.

Preheat oven to 425 degrees F.

On a lightly floured surface, roll out the larger ball of dough into a 12-inch round. Ease dough into a deep 9-inch pie plate. Brush bottom of dough with preserves. (If preserves are too thick to brush onto dough, thin with a few drops of water or sherry.) Spoon filling into pie shell, distributing it evenly.

Roll smaller pastry ball into an 11-inch round. Using a sharp knife, cut pastry into ½-inch-wide strips. (You should have about 14 strips.) Weave pastry strips into a lattice over top of pie by placing a strip at the edge of the pie, then placing a second strip at right angles to the first, and continuing to alternate strips in this manner until pie is covered. Press pastry strips firmly in place at edge of pie and flute or crimp pastry all around rim. Brush lattice and edge of pastry with cream. Sprinkle lattice with sugar. Cover crimped edge of pie loosely with aluminum foil. Bake in lower third of oven for 30 minutes.

Remove foil from edge. Reduce oven temperature to 400 degrees F., and continue to bake pie for 15 to 20 minutes, or until pastry is a rich golden brown and filling is bubbly.

— MAKES ONE 9-INCH PIE —

You can also omit the lattice top for the pie and make a glossy fruit glaze instead with any of the "fruit only" conserves. Stir 1 tablespoon cornstarch into 1 tablespoon cold water and combine with 1 jar of "fruit only" conserve. In a small saucepan, heat the mixture gently until it bubbles slightly and loses its cloudiness. Bake the peach pie without the lattice top and let it cool. Then gently spread the thickened compote over the filling. Let the pie and glaze cool and serve with lightly whipped cream.

HARVEST MOON

M E N U

◆

*T*OMATO AND CELERY
SOUP

◆

*G*LAZED PORK LOIN
WITH GARLIC POTATOES

◆

*B*RUSSELS SPROUTS IN
BROWN BUTTER

◆

*A*PPLE-QUINCE BREAD
PUDDING

OPPOSITE: GLAZED PORK LOIN WITH
GARLIC POTATOES

TOMATO AND CELERY SOUP

THIS FRESH-FLAVORED SOUP MAKES A LIGHT, COLORFUL FIRST COURSE for a substantial dinner.

4½ tablespoons butter
3   large ribs celery, with leaves, coarsely diced
3¾ pounds fresh tomatoes, unpeeled, halved, and
    seeded
4½ cups chicken stock
⅔   cup dry white wine
1   bay leaf
1½ tablespoons minced marjoram leaves, or ¾
    teaspoon dried
¾   teaspoon celery seed
¼   teaspoon sugar
4   sprigs fresh parsley
¾   teaspoon Worcestershire sauce
3   dashes Tabasco
    Salt
    Freshly ground black pepper

TO SERVE
Fresh celery leaves

This combination, as delicious cold as hot, becomes a textured aspic when gelatin is added. Soften 2 envelopes un-flavored gelatin (about 2 tablespoons total) in ½ cup cold water and stir the mixture into the hot soup. Pour the soup mixture into an oiled 2-quart mold and let it cool. Chill the mixture until it is set. Turn the aspic out onto a decorative dish. If using a ring mold, fill the center with a poultry, fish, or rice salad or a bunch of watercress sprigs; if molded into a solid shape, surround with the salad.

In a 4-quart, heavy, non-reactive saucepan, melt the butter, add celery, and cook over medium-low heat for about 4 minutes, or until celery is softened but not browned. Add tomatoes, stock, wine, bay leaf, marjoram, celery seed, sugar, and parsley. Stir well and bring to a boil. Lower heat and simmer gently, uncovered, for 15 to 20 minutes, or until the celery is very soft. Stir in Worcestershire sauce and Tabasco, discard bay leaf, and let soup cool slightly.

Turn soup into a food processor and process with on/off motion until soup is a coarse purée with bite-size pieces of celery and tomato still visible. Season to taste with salt and pepper. Return soup to the saucepan and simmer over medium heat until hot. Ladle into individual soup bowls and garnish each serving with celery leaves. Or transfer to a large tureen, sprinkle soup with celery leaves, and serve.

— 6 SERVINGS —

APPLE-QUINCE BREAD PUDDING

IF QUINCES ARE NOT AVAILABLE, SUBSTITUTE A SECOND apple.

10 to 12 slices day-old firm white bread, crusts removed
4 large eggs
2 cups heavy cream
½ cup milk
4 tablespoons honey
2 teaspoons vanilla extract
1 large Golden Delicious apple
1 ripe quince
¼ cup plus 1 tablespoon sugar
1½ teaspoons fresh lemon juice

TO SERVE
Crabtree & Evelyn Honey & Ginger Sauce (optional)

Cut bread into 1-inch cubes. (There should be about 5 cups.)

In a large mixing bowl, beat eggs lightly. Beat in cream, milk, honey, and vanilla. Add bread cubes and stir gently. Cover loosely and set aside to soak for 1 to 2 hours.

Preheat oven to 325 degrees F.

Peel, core, and thinly slice apple and quince. In a small mixing bowl, combine fruit with ¼ cup of the sugar and the lemon juice and toss until fruit is coated. Fold fruit into soaked bread, turning gently with a spatula until combined.

Spoon mixture into a lightly buttered, shallow 2-quart baking dish and smooth top with a spatula. Bake in the center of oven for 35 minutes.

Sprinkle top of pudding with remaining 1 tablespoon sugar and continue baking for about 10 minutes, or until top of pudding is golden brown and a knife inserted 2 inches from the edge comes out clean. (The center of the pudding will still be slightly runny; it will finish cooking after being removed from oven.) If top of pudding has not formed a golden brown crust, place pudding under preheated broiler for 30 to 60 seconds, or until browned.

Serve warm, accompanied by Honey & Ginger Sauce if desired. Or prepare up to 2 hours ahead and serve tepid.

— 6 SERVINGS —

This can also be served with a purée made by stewing dried apricots in water to cover, then blending the apricots in a food processor with enough of the juices to give the consistency of heavy cream. Sharpen the flavor with a spoonful or so of kirsch, if desired.

GLAZED PORK LOIN
WITH GARLIC POTATOES

MEAT AND POTATOES ROASTED TOGETHER ARE ALWAYS DELICIOUS. IN this recipe, the two main ingredients are given their own individual seasoning during the last half hour of cooking: a mustard glaze for the pork loin, and garlic for the potatoes. Crabtree & Evelyn Cumberland Sauce may be used in place of the red currant jelly.

1 pork loin (about 5 pounds), chine bone removed or sawed through to facilitate carving and meat tied at intervals with string
  Salt
  Freshly ground pepper
18 small new red potatoes
3 tablespoons red currant jelly
2 teaspoons minced fresh rosemary, or ¾ teaspoon dried
¾ cup dry white wine
2 to 3 teaspoons Champagne-flavored or Dijon-style mustard
1 clove garlic, chopped

TO SERVE
Fresh rosemary sprigs

Preheat oven to 325 degrees F.

Sprinkle pork loin with salt and pepper and place on a rack in a shallow roasting pan. Bake in the center of oven for 2 to 2½ hours (about 25 to 30 minutes per pound), or until a meat thermometer inserted into the center of roast registers 165 degrees F.

Bring a large saucepan of lightly salted water to a boil. If potatoes are very small, leave them whole and peel away a thin band of skin around the middle of each. If using larger potatoes, do not peel, but cut into 2-inch cubes. Cook in boiling water until almost tender, about 10 minutes, and drain thoroughly in a colander.

When roast has cooked for about 1 hour, add potatoes to the roasting pan, turning them in the pan juices to coat well. Turn potatoes occasionally during roasting so that they brown evenly.

In a small saucepan, combine jelly, rosemary, and 2 tablespoons of the wine and warm over low heat until the jelly melts. Stir in mustard.

About ½ hour before roast is finished cooking, brush glaze over pork. Brush with glaze every 10 minutes.

About 10 minutes before roast has finished cooking, sprinkle garlic over the potatoes.

When the internal temperature of the roast has reached 165 degrees F., remove meat to a cutting board, and allow it to rest for 15 minutes before carving. Remove potatoes from the roasting pan and keep warm.

Skim fat from the juices in the roasting pan. Stir in remaining wine and boil sauce on top of stove for 2 or 3 minutes.

Carve meat downward next to the bone (if it has not been removed) and arrange slices on a serving platter. Surround with the potatoes and garnish with rosemary sprigs. Turn sauce into a sauce boat and pass with the pork.

— 6 SERVINGS —

$\mathscr{B}$RUSSELS SPROUTS IN BROWN BUTTER

THE BUTTER CAN BE BROWNED IN ADVANCE AND RE-HEATED WHEN the sprouts are draining.

    2   pounds fresh Brussels sprouts (35 to 40)
    6   tablespoons unsalted butter
    1   tablespoon fresh lemon juice
        Salt
        Freshly ground pepper

Discard tough and damaged outer leaves from sprouts. Trim away fibrous ends of stems, being careful not to cut away too much.

Bring a large pot of lightly salted water to a boil over high heat, add sprouts, boil for 7 to 8 minutes, or until just tender, and drain.

Meanwhile, in a large saucepan melt butter over medium heat and cook until it turns a deep golden brown, 3 to 4 minutes, being very careful not to let it burn.

Add Brussels sprouts along with lemon juice to saucepan and toss gently in the brown butter. Season with salt and a generous grinding of pepper, toss well, and serve.

— 6 SERVINGS —

Elevate Brussels sprouts into an even more elegant vegetable by puréeing them. In a food processor, purée the boiled, drained sprouts to a coarse consistency. Stir in the butter and lemon juice and add ¼ cup light cream to smooth the consistency slightly. Reheat before serving and sprinkle with ¼ cup crumbled bacon.

CHRISTMAS FEAST

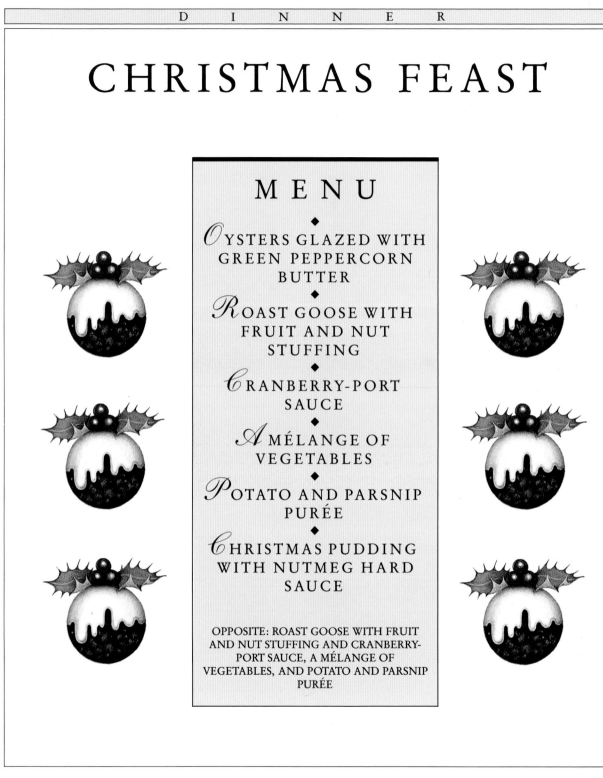

M E N U

◆

*O*YSTERS GLAZED WITH
GREEN PEPPERCORN
BUTTER

◆

*R*OAST GOOSE WITH
FRUIT AND NUT
STUFFING

◆

*C*RANBERRY-PORT
SAUCE

◆

A MÉLANGE OF
VEGETABLES

◆

*P*OTATO AND PARSNIP
PURÉE

◆

*C*HRISTMAS PUDDING
WITH NUTMEG HARD
SAUCE

OPPOSITE: ROAST GOOSE WITH FRUIT
AND NUT STUFFING AND CRANBERRY-
PORT SAUCE, A MÉLANGE OF
VEGETABLES, AND POTATO AND PARSNIP
PURÉE

Oysters Glazed with Green Peppercorn Butter

THIS MAKES A LIGHT BUT ELEGANT STARTER FOR CHRISTMAS DINNER. The peppercorn butter can be made a couple of days ahead and kept in the refrigerator or frozen earlier still. Bring it to room temperature before using.

GREEN PEPPERCORN BUTTER
½ cup (1 stick) unsalted butter, softened
2 tablespoons chopped fresh parsley
1 tablespoon chopped shallot
1 tablespoon fresh lemon juice
1 teaspoon crushed dried green peppercorns
  Pinch cayenne
¼ teaspoon salt
  Freshly ground black pepper

2 dozen fresh oysters in the shells
  Coarse salt
¾ cup fresh bread crumbs made from day-old bread

Combine butter, parsley, shallot, lemon juice, peppercorns, cayenne, salt, and black pepper in a food processor, blender, or large mixing bowl and blend or beat together. Taste for seasoning and add more salt if necessary.

Preheat broiler.

Shuck oysters, discarding top half of each shell. Loosen each from bottom half of shell, wiping away any sand or grit, and replace on bottom half of shell. Spread a generous layer of coarse salt over a baking sheet, an ovenproof serving platter, or individual ovenproof plates. Arrange oysters on coarse salt.

Spread about 1½ teaspoons green peppercorn butter over top of each oyster, then sprinkle each with 1½ teaspoons bread crumbs. Broil oysters under hot broiler about 4 inches from the heat for about 3 minutes, or until butter is sizzling, crumbs are golden, and oysters are plumped and beginning to curl around edges. Serve hot.

— 6 FIRST-COURSE SERVINGS —

A MÉLANGE OF VEGETABLES

EARLY IN THE DAY, SLICE THE CABBAGE AND COVER IT WITH WATER acidulated with 2 teaspoons vinegar or fresh lemon juice to hold the color. (Before the final cooking, drain the cabbage well and shake it in a clean dish cloth until almost dry.) The carrots and beans can be steamed ahead of time, too. The dish should be completed just before serving, but the cooking time is only about 5 minutes.

This recipe provides generous servings, and any that is left over is delicious reheated.

4 carrots (about ¾ pound), scraped and thinly sliced diagonally
1 pound thin green beans, trimmed and sliced diagonally into 2-inch lengths
½ cup (1 stick) unsalted butter
2 tablespoons herb-flavored white-wine vinegar or sherry vinegar
½ small head red cabbage (about 12 ounces), thinly sliced
1 tablespoon Crabtree & Evelyn Provençal Herbs Mustard or Dijon-style mustard
   Salt
   Freshly ground pepper

Steam carrots and beans in a steamer basket over a pan of boiling water about 2 minutes, or until crisp-tender. Refresh under cold water to stop cooking and set color.

Melt butter in a large skillet over medium-low heat until it foams. When foam subsides, stir in vinegar. Add cabbage and toss over medium-high heat for about 2 minutes, or until it is crisp-tender.

Stir in mustard, carrots, and beans and sauté, tossing, until all vegetables are hot, about 1 minute. Season with salt and pepper. Serve immediately.

— 8 SERVINGS —

ROAST GOOSE WITH FRUIT AND NUT STUFFING

GOOSE HAS A LONG TRADITION AS A CHRISTMAS ROAST, AND A NATU-rally reared one is much sought after for the flavor and quality of its meat. It is hardly the meatiest of birds, but as the carcass makes a very fine stock and the fat an excellent frying medium, goose contributes to several meals of good eating.

The day before, the stuffing can be nearly completed, the goose cleaned, and the giblet stock for the gravy prepared, leaving only the final assembly and roasting for Christmas Day.

1	fresh goose (10 to 12 pounds)
½	lemon
	Salt
	Freshly ground pepper
	Fruit and Nut Stuffing (page 208)
1	cup dry red wine
4	whole black peppercorns
2	sprigs fresh parsley
½	rib celery, sliced
1	small onion, coarsely chopped
1	bay leaf
3	tablespoons Madeira or medium Sherry

The fruit and nut stuffing may be modified and is delicious in a turkey of the same size as the goose. Increase the quantity of butter to 12 tablespoons (1½ sticks) and cook ½ pound diced smoked or unsmoked bacon with the onions and celery to introduce a rich moistness that counteracts the relative dryness of the turkey.

Remove giblets and neck from goose cavity and set aside. Rinse cavity and skin of goose and pat dry. Rub goose skin with cut side of lemon half. Season inside and out with salt and pepper. Prick goose skin all over without piercing the meat.

Preheat oven to 425 degrees F.

Stuff goose cavity loosely with fruit and nut stuffing. Turn goose and loosely stuff neck. Securely truss cavity and neck and roast goose, breast side up, on a rack in a shallow roasting pan in center of oven for 20 minutes. Reduce oven temperature to 350 degrees F., turn goose breast side down, and continue roasting for 1 hour. Use a baster or spoon to remove excess fat from roasting pan about 3 times during roasting (see Note). Turn goose breast side up again and continue roasting 1 hour, or until meat thermometer inserted into breast registers 175 degrees F. Increase oven temperature to 450 degrees F. and roast 20 minutes more to crisp skin.

While goose is roasting, in a large saucepan combine giblets and neck with 4 cups water, ½ cup of the wine, the peppercorns, parsley, celery, onion, and bay leaf, partially cover, and simmer over low heat for 1½ to 2 hours, or until liquid is reduced to about 1½ cups. Strain stock into a bowl.

Transfer goose to a warmed carving platter and let it rest about 15 minutes before carving. Meanwhile, pour off excess fat from roasting pan. Add Madeira to pan juices, scraping up brown bits, stir in goose stock and remaining ½ cup wine, and simmer in roasting pan over low heat for about 10 minutes, or until reduced to about 1½ cups. Season with salt and pepper.

Remove stuffing from goose and place in a serving dish. Carve goose and serve, accompanied by stuffing and gravy.

— 6 TO 8 SERVINGS —

CRANBERRY-PORT SAUCE

THIS SAUCE CAN BE MADE A FEW DAYS IN ADVANCE AND STORED IN THE refrigerator. Bring to room temperature before serving.

1   pound fresh cranberries
¾   cup Port
½   cup sugar
¼   cup orange juice
1   tablespoon grated orange zest
     a ¼-inch-thick slice of fresh gingerroot
2   tablespoons red currant jelly

In a large enamel or other non-reactive saucepan, combine cranberries, Port, sugar, orange juice, orange zest, and gingerroot. Bring to a boil over medium-high heat, stirring to dissolve sugar. Reduce heat to low and simmer for 12 to 15 minutes, stirring frequently, until cranberries have popped and the sauce is slightly thickened. Discard gingerroot, stir in jelly, and set aside to cool. Serve at room temperature with roast fowl.

— MAKES ABOUT 3 CUPS SAUCE —

The copious amount of fat that runs from even a modest goose as it cooks is one of the tastiest and best frying fats, particularly for searing meats and sautéeing potatoes and onions.

To keep it, heat the fat until liquid, then strain it through several thicknesses of cheesecloth into jars. Covered and refrigerated, it will keep well for several months.

A flavorful sauce can also be made simply by combining 1 tablespoon grated orange zest, 1 teaspoon freshly grated gingerroot, and 1 or 2 teaspoons Port with a jar of Crabtree & Evelyn Wild Cranberry Sauce.

FRUIT AND NUT STUFFING

½ cup quartered pitted dried prunes
½ cup quartered dried apricots
¼ cup Madeira or medium Sherry
½ cup broken walnuts
½ cup coarsely chopped blanched almonds
2 tablespoons butter
1 large onion, chopped
1 rib celery, chopped
1 tart apple, peeled, cored, and coarsely chopped
1 firm ripe pear, peeled, cored, and coarsely chopped
⅓ cup seeded and coarsely chopped fresh kumquats,
including skin (see Note)
4 tablespoons chopped fresh parsley
1 teaspoon grated orange zest
1 teaspoon dried sage
½ teaspoon dried thyme
⅛ teaspoon ground cinnamon
¼ teaspoon ground mace
Pinch ground coriander seed
1 teaspoon salt
¼ teaspoon freshly ground pepper
3 cups cubed day-old whole-wheat bread

This can be prepared a day ahead to the point of adding the bread cubes and macerated fruit, nuts, and lightly cooked ingredients.

The night before assembling stuffing, combine prunes, apricots, and Madeira in a bowl and let fruit macerate overnight.

Preheat oven to 350 degrees F.

Spread walnuts and almonds on a baking sheet and toast in oven for 5 to 10 minutes, or until lightly browned and fragrant.

Melt butter in a large skillet. Add onion and celery and cook over low heat for about 2 minutes. Add apple and pear and cook about 3 minutes more, or until vegetables and fruit are softened. Remove skillet from heat and stir in kumquats, parsley, orange zest, sage, thyme, cinnamon, mace, coriander seed, salt, and pepper. Add bread cubes, chopped nuts, and macerated dried fruit with its liquid and toss until well blended.

— MAKES ABOUT 7 CUPS, ENOUGH TO STUFF A 10- TO 12-POUND BIRD —

Note: If kumquats are unavailable, substitute Crabtree & Evelyn Orange Fruit Only Conserve or Black Currant Fruit Only Conserve.

Potato and Parsnip Purée

To simplify the cooking on Christmas Day, the potatoes and parsnips can be peeled and cut, ready for cooking, the day before. Put them in bowls or saucepans and cover with cold water.

2   pounds white potatoes, peeled and quartered
¾   pound parsnips, peeled and cut into large pieces
½   cup (1 stick) butter
½   cup finely chopped green onions (white and some green)
½   to 1 cup milk, heated
    Salt
    Freshly ground pepper
2   tablespoons chopped fresh parsley
2   tablespoons chopped fresh chives

TO SERVE
Several chive blades

Bring a large pot of lightly salted water to a boil over high heat, add potatoes, and boil for 10 minutes. Add parsnips and boil 10 minutes more, or until parsnips and potatoes are tender.

Meanwhile, melt butter in a small saucepan over low heat. Add green onions and cook over medium-low heat until softened, about 2 minutes.

Drain potatoes and parsnips, return them to pot, and heat for about 1 minute, tossing to let all excess moisture evaporate.

Pass potatoes and parsnips through a ricer or food mill, or mash with a masher. Slowly stir in ½ cup milk and blend well. If too thick, add additional milk. Beat in green onion mixture, season with salt and pepper, and blend in parsley and chopped chives.

To serve, spoon mixture into a serving dish and arrange 2-inch lengths of chive blades in a fan shape on top.

— 8 SERVINGS —

CHRISTMAS PUDDING WITH NUTMEG HARD·SAUCE

THESE PUDDINGS ARE ALWAYS BEST WHEN MADE SEVERAL WEEKS ahead—at least—to allow the flavor to develop. Wrap the steamed pudding in brandy-soaked cheesecloth and foil and store it in a cool, dry place. To reheat it, remove the foil and cheesecloth, place the pudding back in its mold, and steam for about 1 hour. Or rewrap it in foil and warm it in a low oven for about 45 minutes.

½ cup flour
1 teaspoon ground cinnamon
½ teaspoon baking soda
½ teaspoon salt
¼ teaspoon ground cloves
¼ teaspoon ground nutmeg
¼ teaspoon ground mace
½ cup ground beef suet (see Note), softened
⅔ cup firmly packed light brown sugar
3 large eggs
3 tablespoons plum preserves
1 tablespoon grated orange zest
¾ cup dry bread crumbs
1 cup chopped dried figs
1 cup coarsely chopped pecans
½ cup chopped dates
⅓ cup currants
⅓ cup raisins
⅓ cup golden raisins
¼ cup chopped citron
¼ cup chopped candied orange peel
¼ cup chopped candied lemon peel
¼ cup chopped crystallized gingerroot
Nutmeg Hard Sauce (recipe follows)

Sift together flour, cinnamon, baking soda, salt, cloves, nutmeg, and mace onto a sheet of waxed paper.

In a large mixing bowl, beat suet until as creamy as possible. Add brown sugar and beat thoroughly. Add eggs, one at a time, beating well after each addition. (Mixture may look curdled at this point.) Beat in plum preserves and orange zest. Add flour mixture and bread crumbs and beat until well blended. Stir in figs, pecans, dates, currants, raisins, citron, orange peel, lemon peel, and gingerroot.

Spoon batter into a 2-quart pudding mold that has been well buttered (including lid) and sprinkled lightly with granulated sugar. Cover mold tightly with lid and set on a wire rack in a large pot. Pour in enough boiling water to come about halfway up side of pudding mold. Cover pot tightly and steam pudding over very low heat for 3½ to 4½ hours, or until a skewer inserted into the center of pudding comes out clean.

Remove pudding mold from pot and let pudding cool 10 minutes in the mold. Carefully unmold pudding and wrap in brandy-soaked cheesecloth and foil and store in a cool, dry place. When ready to serve, reheat, slice pudding into ½-inch-thick slices, and serve with Nutmeg Hard Sauce.

— 8 TO 10 SERVINGS —

Note: Ground suet is available during the holidays in supermarkets. Otherwise, have the butcher grind it.

$\mathcal{N}$UTMEG HARD SAUCE

THIS SAUCE CAN BE MADE A FEW DAYS AHEAD AND STORED IN THE refrigerator. Bring to room temperature before serving, and, if necessary, beat sauce briefly to return it to a light, fluffy consistency.

½ cup (1 stick) unsalted butter, softened
1½ cups powdered sugar
¼ cup Cognac or other brandy
½ teaspoon freshly grated nutmeg
½ teaspoon vanilla extract
   Pinch salt
2 tablespoons heavy cream

   TO SERVE
   Freshly grated nutmeg

In a mixing bowl, cream together butter and sugar until very light and fluffy. Add Cognac, nutmeg, vanilla, and salt and beat until very light. If sauce seems too stiff, slowly add up to 2 tablespoons cream.

Spoon sauce into a small serving dish and grate a little nutmeg over top. Serve with Christmas pudding.

— MAKES ¾ CUP SAUCE —

For a highly effective, deceptively easy Christmas dessert, crumble leftover plum pudding (or a whole small pudding) and fold it into high-quality bought or homemade vanilla ice cream. A tablespoonful of brandy will also enhance the flavor.

DINNER FOR A FAVORITE UNCLE

M E N U

◆

*F*OIE GRAS SALAD WITH
COGNAC VINAIGRETTE

◆

*B*RAISED VEAL WITH
COARSE-GRAINED
MUSTARD SAUCE

◆

*P*URÉE OF BROCCOLI
AND PEAS

◆

*W*ILD RICE AND GRAPES

◆

*C*HOCOLATE ALMOND
CAKE WITH RUM CREAM

OPPOSITE: CHOCOLATE ALMOND CAKE
WITH RUM CREAM

ℱOIE GRAS SALAD WITH COGNAC VINAIGRETTE

THE COGNAC VINAIGRETTE MAY BE PREPARED IN ADVANCE AND RE-frigerated until needed. Bring to room temperature and whisk to blend just before serving. The salads may be assembled ahead up to the point of adding the *foie gras* and dressing and refrigerated until serving time.

COGNAC VINAIGRETTE

2 tablespoons olive oil
2 shallots, minced
3 tablespoons Cognac or other brandy
3 tablespoons red-wine vinegar
1 teaspoon Dijon-style mustard
⅔ cup vegetable oil
1 tablespoon walnut oil
¾ teaspoon salt
⅛ teaspoon freshly ground pepper

SALAD

30 *haricots verts*, thin green beans, or pencil-thin asparagus spears
1 small head chicory (curly endive), torn into pieces
1 bunch arugula, tough ends trimmed
½ sweet red pepper, cored, seeded, and cut into thin strips
2 ounces fresh or canned cooked *foie gras*

In a small skillet, combine olive oil and shallots and cook over medium heat for 1 minute. Remove skillet from heat, add Cognac, and let it warm in the hot pan for a few seconds. Carefully light Cognac with a match and allow the alcohol to burn off, gently shaking skillet until flames die out. Pour shallot mixture into a mixing bowl and allow to cool slightly. Add vinegar and mustard and whisk to blend. Gradually whisk in vegetable and walnut oils until a thick vinaigrette forms. Add salt and pepper and whisk to blend.

Trim off stem ends of beans. If using asparagus, trim off all but 2½ inches of tips, reserving the remaining portion of spears for another use. Plunge beans or asparagus tips into a large saucepan of rapidly boiling water and blanch for 2 minutes. Drain in a colander, refresh under cold water to stop cooking, and drain again.

Divide chicory and arugula leaves among 6 individual salad plates. Arrange beans or asparagus and red pepper over greens.

Just before serving, cut the *foie gras* into 6 thin slices and place one slice in the center of each salad. Drizzle about 2 tablespoons Cognac vinaigrette over each serving.

Serve immediately.

— 6 SERVINGS —

*W*ILD RICE AND GRAPES

THIS IS AN ESPECIALLY GOOD COMBINATION; BUT, IF WILD RICE IS unavailable, natural brown rice may be used instead.

1½ cups wild rice
4   tablespoons butter
½   cup chopped onion
1   teaspoon salt
20 seedless green grapes, halved
20 purple grapes, halved and, if necessary, seeded
¼   cup minced fresh parsley
    Freshly ground pepper

Rinse the rice thoroughly in a colander and let drain.

In a large heavy saucepan or skillet with a lid, melt 3 tablespoons of the butter. Add onion and cook over low heat for 3 to 4 minutes, or until softened. Add rice and toss to coat with butter. Stir in 3 cups water and the salt. Bring to a simmer, cover tightly, and cook over low heat, stirring occasionally, for 45 to 50 minutes, or until rice is tender and all water is absorbed. If water is absorbed before rice is tender, add a few tablespoons more and continue cooking.

Melt the remaining tablespoon butter in a medium skillet. Add green and purple grapes and toss in the butter until heated through. Add grape mixture and parsley to the cooked wild rice, season with pepper, and toss to mix thoroughly. Add additional salt if necessary. Serve hot.

— 6 GENEROUS SERVINGS —

BRAISED VEAL WITH COARSE-GRAINED MUSTARD SAUCE

ASK THE BUTCHER TO SAVE THE BONES FROM THE VEAL LOIN AND TIE them to the bottom of loin to act as a rack during braising and to flavor the sauce. Or ask for about 2 pounds small veal bones and simply add them to the roasting pan to cook with veal loin.

A piece of pork loin could be used in place of the veal, but the cooking time should then be increased by half an hour. The full-bodied but not overwhelming sauce is a fine foil to the delicate taste of the meat.

1	3-pound boneless loin of veal, tied with string, plus about 2 pounds veal bones
	Salt
	Freshly ground pepper
3	tablespoons plus 4 teaspoons butter
3	tablespoons vegetable oil
½	cup finely diced carrot
½	cup finely diced celery
½	cup finely diced leek
½	cup finely diced onion
¼	cup Port
1½	cups dry white wine
1	bouquet garni composed of 1 parsley sprig, 1 bay leaf, ¼ teaspoon dried marjoram, 1 teaspoon dried rosemary, and ¼ teaspoon dried thyme, all tied together in a square of cheesecloth
1	tablespoon plus 1 teaspoon all-purpose flour
2	teaspoons coarse-grained mustard

Pat veal loin dry and season lightly with salt and pepper. Place 4 teaspoons of the butter in a small bowl and reserve to soften.

Preheat oven to 375 degrees F.

In a large skillet, melt 1 tablespoon of the remaining butter with 1 tablespoon oil. Add carrot, celery, leek, and onion and cook over low heat until softened, about 10 minutes. Using a slotted spoon, transfer vegetables to a roasting pan or ovenproof casserole.

In the skillet, melt the 2 tablespoons remaining butter with the 2 remaining tablespoons oil. Add veal loin and brown over medium-high heat until well-browned on all sides. Place meat on bed of cooked vegetables in roasting pan.

Any leftover veal can be thinly sliced and served at room temperature with a simple tuna mayonnaise for a quickly made version of the classic vitello tonnato. Combine a 3-ounce can tuna, drained, in a food processor or blender with 1 cup good-quality mayonnaise, 3 flat anchovy fillets, and 3 tablespoons heavy cream. Blend the mixture until smooth, thinning it to the consistency of light cream with a few spoonfuls dry white wine, and then season to taste with lemon juice and cayenne. Arrange the sliced veal on a serving dish, spoon the sauce over it, and sprinkle 2 tablespoons drained capers on top.

Pour Port into skillet and reduce, scraping up any brown bits, over medium-high heat to about 2 tablespoons. Pour Port mixture over veal loin. Add wine, bouquet garni, and 1½ cups water. (If veal bones were not tied to the loin, add them to the roasting pan at this point.)

Cover roasting pan tightly with a lid or heavy-duty aluminum foil. Place in the center of oven and immediately reduce oven temperature to 325 degrees F. Cook for 1¼ to 1½ hours (about 30 minutes per pound), or until a meat thermometer inserted in center of meat registers 175 degrees F.

Discard bones and bouquet garni. Transfer meat to a serving platter and keep warm while preparing sauce.

Pour juices from roasting pan into a large saucepan, skim off fat, and bring juices to a simmer. Cook over high heat, skimming off fat and particles that rise to the surface, until sauce is reduced and thickened slightly, about 10 minutes.

Meanwhile, blend flour and mustard into the 4 teaspoons reserved softened butter. Whisk this *beurre manié*, ½ teaspoon at a time, into the sauce and simmer for 3 to 4 minutes more to completely cook flour and thicken sauce. Taste and season, if necessary, with salt and pepper.

Remove trussing strings from meat and slice into ⅜-inch-thick slices. Spoon some of the sauce over meat slices. Serve remaining sauce in a sauce boat.

— 6 SERVINGS —

MADE IN FRANCE

GREEN PEPPER SAUCE

CRABTREE & EVELYN
LONDON

250 ml
8.8 fl oz

PURÉE OF BROCCOLI AND PEAS

Although the food processor allows every cook to make vegetable purées as smooth as cream in a matter of seconds, those with a bit of texture remaining are often more interesting.

THE PURÉE CAN BE MADE EARLY IN THE DAY AND REHEATED JUST before serving. Leftovers may be heated in good-quality clear stock or broth to make an attractive and tasty soup.

1   large bunch broccoli (about 2 pounds)
10 ounces frozen peas (1½ cups)
6   tablespoons butter
¼   cup heavy cream
1   teaspoon salt
⅛   teaspoon freshly ground pepper
    Pinch nutmeg

Trim off and discard tough ends of broccoli and cut broccoli into 1-inch pieces. Bring a large saucepan or stock pot of lightly salted water to a boil, add broccoli, and boil until almost tender, about 8 minutes. Add peas and boil with broccoli another 4 to 5 minutes, or until both vegetables are tender. Drain vegetables in a colander.

While vegetables are still warm, purée them (in 2 batches if necessary) in a food processor with the butter and cream, using an on/off motion, until mixture is smooth but retains textured flecks of each vegetable. Return purée to saucepan, season with salt, pepper, and nutmeg, and stir to blend. Warm gently over low heat and serve.

— 6 SERVINGS —

218

CHOCOLATE ALMOND CAKE WITH RUM CREAM

TAKE CARE NOT TO OVERCOOK THIS LOVELY, ULTRA-MOIST CHOCO-late cake. It is best slightly underdone in the center, and since it contains no raw flour to upset the taste or digestion there's no danger in serving it a little undercooked. It can be made early in the day or a day in advance. Substitute ¾ cup good marmalade for the corn syrup and rum in the cream for a different flavor.

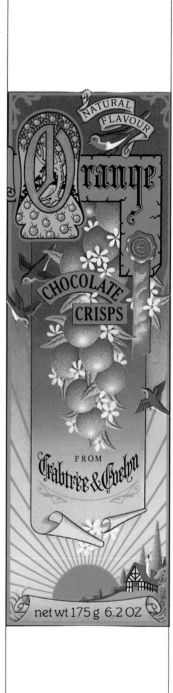

6   ounces semisweet chocolate, broken into chunks
6   tablespoons unsalted butter
¼   cup sugar
3   large eggs, separated
½   cup plus 2 tablespoons ground almonds
¾   cup fine fresh bread crumbs

RUM CREAM
¾   cup heavy cream
3   tablespoons dark corn syrup
¼   cup dark rum

Preheat oven to 375 degrees F.

In a medium saucepan, heat chocolate and butter over very low heat until both are melted. Remove from heat and stir in sugar and egg yolks. Stir in ½ cup of the ground almonds and the bread crumbs.

In a separate bowl, beat egg whites until stiff but not dry. Spoon about a quarter of the chocolate mixture into the whites and fold gently together. Pour in remaining chocolate mixture and fold lightly but thoroughly.

Turn batter into an 8-inch springform cake pan that has been buttered and dusted with the remaining 2 tablespoons ground almonds. Bake in the center of oven for 25 minutes, or until almost, but not quite, set in the middle. Let cool in the pan on a wire rack. (The cake will deflate slightly.)

To make the sauce, whip the cream until stiff peaks form. Stir in the corn syrup and rum. Whip briefly to rethicken cream and serve in a bowl with the cake, or pipe cream decoratively on top of the cake.

— 6 TO 8 SERVINGS —

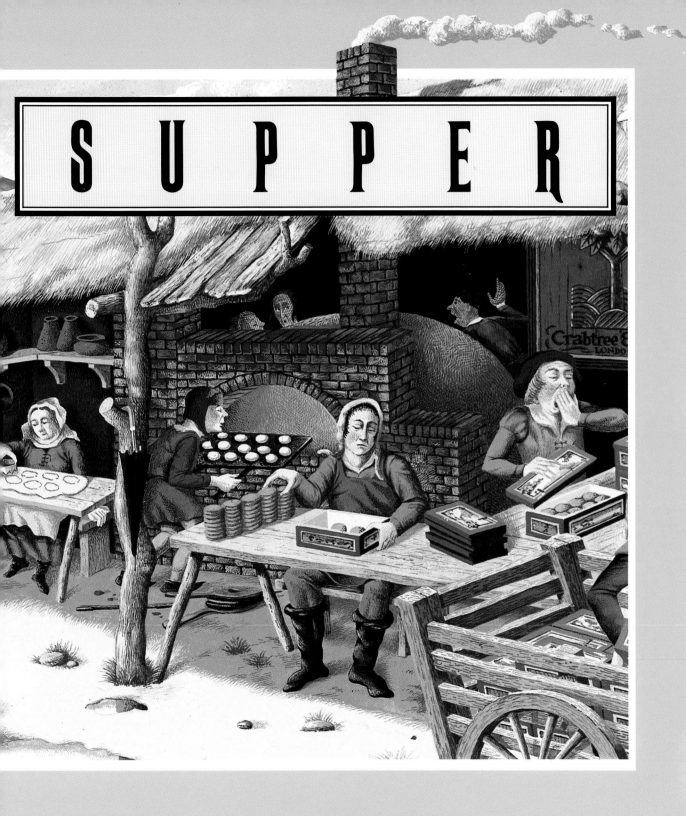

SUPPER

WARM SUMMER'S EVENING

MENU

◆

*B*RIE AND BLUEBERRY
SALAD

◆

*S*HRIMP AND SNOW PEA
PAELLA

◆

*G*RUYÈRE ROLLS
(SEE APPENDIX)

◆

*L*IME SHERBET WITH
CANDIED LIME ZEST

◆

*M*OLASSES-RUM LACE
WAFERS

OPPOSITE: BRIE AND BLUEBERRY SALAD,
SHRIMP AND SNOW PEA PAELLA,
LIME SHERBET WITH CANDIED LIME ZEST,
GRUYÈRE ROLLS, AND MOLASSES-RUM
LACE WAFERS

*S*HRIMP AND SNOW PEA PAELLA

THE FIRST STAGES OF COOKING—TO THE POINT OF ADDING THE tomatoes—may be done early in the day. From that point, the paella can be cooked in a 350-degree F. oven instead of on top of the stove.

Pernod or any other anise spirit or liqueur has an affinity with seafood, as well as with white-meat and game birds. Add it, with discretion, to the pan juices or to a seasoned butter to serve with the fish or meat.

3¼ cups chicken stock
12 saffron threads, crushed
¼ pound chorizo or other spicy pork sausage, sliced into ¼-inch rounds
4 tablespoons olive oil
2 pounds peeled and deveined large uncooked shrimp
  Salt
  Freshly ground black pepper
6 ounces fresh snow peas, trimmed
1 small onion, chopped (about ½ cup)
2 small green onions (whites plus some green), chopped (about ¼ cup)
2 cloves garlic, minced
1½ cups Italian Arborio rice or other short- or medium-grain rice
¾ pound plum tomatoes, peeled, seeded, and chopped (about 1 cup)
1 bay leaf
¼ teaspoon dried red pepper flakes
¼ teaspoon freshly grated lemon zest
½ cup dry white wine
1 tablespoon Pernod or other anise-flavored liqueur
¼ cup minced fresh parsley

In a large saucepan, combine the stock and saffron and bring to a simmer over medium-low heat. Remove pan from heat and cover mixture to keep it warm.

In a 14-inch paella pan or ovenproof skillet, cook chorizo over medium heat for about 5 minutes, or until browned. Remove from skillet and drain on paper towels. Set aside.

Discard excess grease from skillet, add 1 tablespoon of the olive oil, and in it sauté shrimp over medium-high heat until they just begin to turn pink, about 2 minutes. Season with salt and pepper. Using a slotted spoon, remove shrimp from skillet and set aside.

Add 1 tablespoon of remaining oil and snow peas to skillet and sauté over medium-high heat for about 30 seconds. Season with salt and pepper. Remove with a slotted spoon and set aside.

Add the remaining 2 tablespoons oil, the onion, and green onion to skillet and cook onions over medium heat until softened, about 3 minutes. Add garlic and cook about 1 minute more. Stir rice into mixture and cook, stirring until all grains are coated with oil, about 1 minute. Stir in tomatoes, bay leaf, pepper flakes, lemon zest, wine, and 2½ cups of the warm saffron-flavored stock and season with salt and pepper. Bring just to a boil, stirring. Reduce heat to low, cover pan, and simmer for about 15 minutes, or until most of liquid is absorbed. If rice absorbs too much liquid during this time and seems dry, add remaining ¾ cup stock.

Discard bay leaf, sprinkle Pernod and 3 tablespoons of the parsley over rice, and toss gently to distribute evenly. Arrange shrimp, snow peas, and chorizo evenly over top of paella, pressing them gently into the rice, and cook over low heat, covered, for 5 to 10 minutes, or until shrimp and snow peas have finished cooking. Sprinkle with remaining parsley and serve immediately from the paella pan or skillet.

— 6 TO 8 SERVINGS —

$\mathscr{B}$RIE AND BLUEBERRY SALAD

2 tablespoons black currant vinegar
2 teaspoons fresh lemon juice
4 tablespoons hazelnut oil
4 tablespoons light vegetable oil
  Pinch ground nutmeg
  Salt
  Freshly ground pepper
4 cups torn Bibb or Boston lettuce leaves
4 cups torn red-leaf lettuce leaves
2 tablespoons small fresh mint leaves
½ pint fresh blueberries (about 1 cup)
8 thin slices (about 4 ounces) brie, St. André, or
  fresh chèvre (see Note)

In a small bowl, whisk together vinegar, lemon juice, hazelnut oil, vegetable oil, and nutmeg. Season with salt and pepper and whisk until well blended.

In a large salad bowl, toss lettuces and mint leaves with just enough dressing to coat them lightly. Divide greens among 8 chilled salad plates. Scatter about 2 tablespoons blueberries over each salad, and arrange a slice of cheese in the center of each salad. Serve immediately.

— 8 SERVINGS —

Note: If the cheese is reasonably firm, chop it into pieces the size of the berries; if very soft, put a single portion in the center of each salad.

Ideally, salad greens should be washed and dried just before serving, but they can also be prepared earlier in the day. Rinse the leaves quickly in cold water, shake excess moisture from them, and either spin them dry or pat them dry with paper towels or a clean dish towel. Then place each variety in a separate plastic bag, avoiding filling the bags too tightly. Refrigerate the greens until needed.

MOLASSES-RUM LACE WAFERS

A VERY PRETTY ALTERNATIVE TO ROLLING THE COOKIES INTO CYLINDERS is to drape each flat, warm cookie over the bottom of an inverted custard cup, pressing to form a cup shape. The cups may be filled with sherbet, ice cream, or mousse. (For larger cups, use about 1 tablespoon of batter for each cookie, bake only 6 at a time, and increase the baking time to 12 to 14 minutes.) Keep these stored in a tightly covered container and use within a few days.

½ cup (1 stick) unsalted butter
½ cup molasses
⅓ cup firmly packed light brown sugar
⅓ cup granulated sugar
1 cup all-purpose flour
¼ teaspoon ground ginger
1 tablespoon dark rum

Preheat oven to 300 degrees F.

In a large heavy saucepan, heat butter and molasses over low heat, stirring, until butter is melted and mixture is smooth. Remove saucepan from heat, add brown and granulated sugars, and stir until smooth. Stir in flour and ginger, whisking briskly to remove lumps and produce a smooth batter. Stir in rum and let batter cool slightly.

Drop teaspoonsful of batter onto a lightly greased baking sheet, leaving at least 3 inches between each cookie (bake and work with no more than 9 cookies at a time). Bake in center of oven for 10 to 12 minutes, or until cookies have spread to about 3 inches in diameter and are bubbly.

Remove from oven and let cookies cool 1 minute on baking sheet. Then, as quickly as possible, carefully lift each cookie off with a spatula and roll it around a wooden spoon handle to form a neat, evenly rolled cylinder. Place rolls on a wire rack to cool. If the last cookies become too hard to remove from baking sheet and roll, return them to the oven for about 15 seconds to soften. Continue to bake and roll cookies in this manner until all batter is used. Store in a tightly covered container.

— MAKES 2½ TO 3 DOZEN COOKIES —

These are similar to the traditional English brandy snap. For this variation, drape the baked cookies around a wooden spoon handle about ¾ inch in diameter or, using a pastry horn, shape them into cornucopias. Fill the cookies with whipped cream, using a pastry bag or small spoon and allowing the cream to protrude generously at each end. Serve two per person on individual plates and offer slices of fresh juicy fruits, such as pineapple, as an accompaniment.

LIME SHERBET
WITH CANDIED LIME ZEST

A zesting tool is useful for taking zest from limes or other citrus fruits, as the strands are stripped from the fruit easily and with no pith (which is bitter) attached.

SERVE THE SHERBET WITH MOLASSES-RUM LACE WAFERS (PAGE 227), either passed separately or molded into "cups" to hold scoops of sherbet.

The candied lime zest can be prepared up to 2 days in advance and stored in a tightly covered container until needed.

CANDIED LIME ZEST
6 tablespoons fresh lime zest cut into julienne strips
6 tablespoons sugar

LIME SHERBET (SEE NOTE)
1⅓ cups sugar
¾ cup fresh lime juice
2 tablespoons fresh lemon juice
1 large egg white
¼ cup heavy cream, well chilled

Fill half a small saucepan with water and bring to a boil. Add lime zest, blanch for about 25 seconds, and drain. Repeat procedure. Fill saucepan with ¾ cup water, stir in 6 tablespoons sugar, and bring to a boil over low heat, stirring occasionally to dissolve sugar. Stir in blanched lime zest, reduce heat to medium, and simmer until liquid is syrupy and zest is glazed, about 10 minutes. Remove zest from syrup with a fork or slotted spoon and spread in a single layer on a sheet of waxed paper. Let cool completely.

To make sherbet, in a medium saucepan combine 2 cups water with 1⅓ cups sugar and bring to a boil over low heat, stirring occasionally to dissolve sugar. Reduce heat to medium and simmer for about 5 minutes. Remove from heat and let cool completely.

Chop candied lime zest and set 3 tablespoons of it aside for garnish. Place remaining 3 tablespoons candied zest in a large mixing bowl and stir in sugar syrup, lime juice, and lemon juice. Chill in the refrigerator for at least 1 hour.

Pour chilled sherbet mixture into the container of an ice-cream maker and freeze according to manufacturer's directions. About 10 minutes before sherbet is finished, place the egg white in a small bowl and beat with a fork until very frothy. Spoon out about ½ cup of sherbet mixture into the bowl and blend with egg white. Add cream and blend until smooth. Pour this mixture into the ice-cream maker with remaining sherbet and finish freezing (see Note).

Place in your refrigerator freezer for at least 2 hours before serving. (Or store, covered, in freezer for up to 3 days before serving.) To serve, scoop balls of sherbet into individual dishes and sprinkle a generous teaspoon of reserved candied lime zest over each serving.

— 6 TO 8 SERVINGS —

Note: If you do not have an ice-cream maker, the sherbet can be prepared as follows: Pour prepared sherbet mixture into a shallow metal pan and place in the freezer until it becomes slushy and thick. Remove from pan and mix in a food processor, a mixer, or in a bowl by hand for a few seconds. Return sherbet to pan and freeze again until slushy. Repeat mixing and refreezing process. Repeat the mixing a third time, beating in frothy egg white and cream, and return sherbet to pan to freeze until firm. This method will not produce as creamy a sherbet as a machine will, but it works very well.

AFTER THE THEATER

MENU

◆

EGGPLANT, GARLIC, AND SUN-DRIED TOMATO SPREAD

◆

LOBSTER, ASPARAGUS, AND PASTA SALAD

◆

SUMMER PUDDING

OPPOSITE: EGGPLANT, GARLIC, AND SUN-DRIED TOMATO SPREAD WITH PITA, LOBSTER, ASPARAGUS, AND PASTA SALAD, AND SUMMER PUDDING

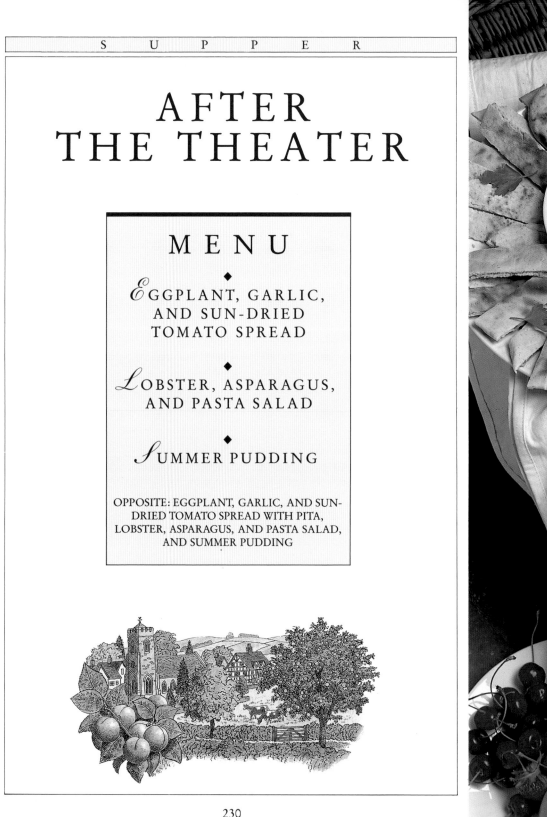

LOBSTER, ASPARAGUS, AND PASTA SALAD

THIS IS A VERY SPECIAL SALAD, WITH MAIN INGREDIENTS WHOSE color, flavor, and texture complement each other beautifully. The dressing can be made a day or two ahead and stored in the refrigerator, and the salad ingredients mixed (but not dressed) several hours in advance.

1 large sweet yellow pepper
1 clove garlic, crushed
1 sprig fresh tarragon, or a pinch dried
  Salt
½ pound thin, tender asparagus spears, trimmed
2 small live lobsters (1 to 1¼ pounds each)
12 ounces rotelle or other spiral-shaped dried pasta
  (about 3 cups)
  Freshly ground black pepper

TARRAGON CREAM DRESSING
3 to 4 tablespoons tarragon white-wine vinegar
1 teaspoon tarragon mustard
¼ cup olive oil
¾ cup heavy cream
1 tablespoon minced chives
3 tablespoons chopped fresh tarragon, or 1
  tablespoon dried
½ teaspoon salt
⅛ teaspoon freshly ground black pepper

TO SERVE
Fresh tarragon sprigs

Roast the sweet pepper by piercing it with a long wooden-handled kitchen fork and holding it over the flame of a gas burner until blackened and charred all over. Or broil pepper on a baking sheet lined with aluminum foil under a hot broiler, turning it occasionally, until all sides are blackened. Drop pepper into a brown paper bag and close tightly, or wrap in aluminum foil, and set aside to steam for about 20 minutes. Holding pepper under cold running water, rub off the blackened skin with your fingers. Drain the pepper and cut it in half horizontally. Remove stem, core, and seeds and cut flesh into ¼-inch strips. Set aside.

To prepare remaining salad ingredients, fill a stock pot large enough to hold the 2 lobsters with water and bring water to a boil. (Do not add lobsters at this point.) Add garlic, tarragon, and 2 to 3 teaspoons salt. Tie asparagus spears together in 2 places with kitchen string and stand the bundle, tip ends up, in the pot. Blanch for about 2 minutes, or until just crisp-tender, remove asparagus bundle, and rinse under cold water to refresh and stop cooking. Drain, cut into 2-inch lengths, and set aside.

Bring water in stock pot back to a rolling boil and carefully lower lobsters into the pot with tongs. Cover pot until water has returned to a boil. Remove cover and cook at a rapid boil for 10 minutes. Remove lobsters from the water with tongs and drain them in a colander. Remove the smaller claw from each lobster and return claws to the pot to flavor cooking liquid. Set lobsters aside to cool.

Meanwhile, bring water back to a boil, skimming off any foam that rises to the surface. Add rotelle to the water, bring back to a boil, and cook until pasta is tender but still firm, or *al dente*, about 8 minutes. Drain in a colander and rinse quickly under cold water to stop cooking. Set aside.

This salad is as versatile as it is delicious, and, should the weather turn cold, it can be made as a hot dish.

Prepare the lobster, asparagus, sweet pepper, and sauce as described, but cook the pasta just before serving time. When the pasta has been drained, turn it back into the pan with 3 table-spoons olive oil and the lobster, asparagus, and pepper. Warm the sauce without letting it boil. Transfer the pasta mix-ture to a heated serving dish, pour the sauce over it, and serve imme-diately.

Crack lobster shells gently and remove meat from the tail of each in one piece, if possible. Carefully crack two remaining claws and try to remove claw meat intact. Set the most attractive claw meat aside to decorate pasta. Chop remaining claw meat into ¾-inch pieces. Slice tail meat crosswise into ¼-inch-thick medallions.

In a large mixing bowl, combine lobster meat, pasta, asparagus, and yellow pepper strips and toss to mix. Cover and refrigerate until just before serving.

To prepare dressing, in a small bowl whisk together vinegar and mustard and slowly whisk in oil and cream. Stir in chives, chopped tarragon, salt, and pepper. Place in a covered container and refrigerate.

Just before serving time, pour dressing over salad and toss gently until well mixed. Arrange on a rimmed serving platter or in a shallow bowl. Garnish with the reserved claw meat and tarragon sprigs.

— 4 SERVINGS —

CRABTREE & EVELYN

VANILLA
Natural Flavour
- BLACK TEA -

Thé à la Vanille

25 Sachets net wt 50 g 1.75 OZ

This spread also makes an excellent base for a fragrant, warming soup. Mix the full amount into 6 cups good-quality chicken stock, simmer the mixture for 10 minutes, and correct the seasoning. Serve the soup hot with 1 tablespoon grated Parmesan sprinkled over each serving if desired.

$\mathcal{E}$GGPLANT, GARLIC, AND SUN-DRIED TOMATO SPREAD

SUN-DRIED TOMATOES, EITHER PACKED IN OIL OR DRIED, ARE AVAILable in most specialty food shops. The dried ones should be soaked in boiling water to cover for 15 minutes, then drained thoroughly, before using. In either form, sun-dried tomatoes add a robust, smokey taste to this spread. They can be salty, however, so season the mixture with care.

4 cloves garlic, unpeeled	¾ teaspoon sesame oil
1½ tablespoons olive oil	⅛ teaspoon freshly ground
1 medium eggplant	black pepper
(1 to 1½ pounds)	Pinch cayenne
3 tablespoons chopped	Salt
sun-dried tomatoes	
3 tablespoons minced	TO SERVE
parsley	Flat-leaf parsley
2 tablespoons fresh lemon	Lemon slices
juice	Pita bread or crackers

Preheat oven to 400 degrees F.

Brush garlic cloves with ½ tablespoon of the olive oil and wrap them all together loosely in a square of aluminum foil. Pierce skin of the eggplant in several places with a fork. Bake eggplant and garlic package on a rimmed baking sheet or jelly-roll pan in center of oven for 30 minutes, remove garlic from oven, and continue baking eggplant for 40 to 50 minutes, turning it once. Remove eggplant from the oven and let cool slightly. (Both eggplant and garlic should be very soft inside.)

When cool enough to handle, squeeze garlic from the skins into a large bowl and mash with a fork to a purée. Cut eggplant in half lengthwise and scoop out the soft flesh. Chop to a coarse purée and add to bowl. Add sun-dried tomatoes and parsley and toss to blend. Stir in lemon juice, sesame oil, the remaining tablespoon olive oil, black pepper, and cayenne. Taste and season with salt, if necessary. Spoon spread into a serving bowl, cover, and chill for at least 1 hour.

Remove spread from refrigerator well before serving to allow it to return to room temperature. Garnish bowl with parsley and lemon slices. Cut pita bread into wedges, toast it, and arrange around the bowl or on a separate plate.

— MAKES 24 TO 30 HORS D'OEUVRES (ABOUT 1½ CUPS SPREAD) —

SUMMER PUDDING

IN ENGLAND, THE BRIEF MOMENT WHEN STRAWBERRIES, RASPBERRIES, and red currants are all ripe together is the time for the finest of summer puddings. The only imperative for this recipe is that the bread become thoroughly saturated with the fruit juices. The pudding should mellow in the refrigerator for 2 days before serving.

2   cups raspberries
2   cups red currants
2   cups sliced strawberries
½   cup sugar
7   to 9 slices two-day-old white bread

    TO SERVE
1   cup heavy cream or *crème fraîche*

In a large saucepan, combine raspberries, currants, and strawberries with ⅓ cup water, bring to a simmer, and cook over medium-low heat for 5 minutes, stirring once or twice. Add the sugar and stir mixture until sugar is dissolved. Remove from the heat and let cool.

Trim crusts from bread and line the bottom and side of a 1-quart mixing bowl with the bread slices, cutting them to fit the bowl neatly.

Pour fruit and most of the juices into the lined bowl and top with a layer of bread cut to fit diameter of bowl. Spoon remaining juice over bread. Invert a plate small enough to fit just inside bowl over top of bread and weight it with a 2-pound weight. Place bowl on a dinner plate and refrigerate for 2 days.

To serve, remove weight and plate from pudding and run a knife around the inside of the bowl to loosen. Carefully invert pudding onto a serving platter. Spoon any juices from bowl or dinner plate over top of the pudding. Serve accompanied by a pitcher of cream or a bowl of *crème fraîche*.

— 4 SERVINGS —

This combination of fruits can also be turned into a popular Scandinavian dessert. When the fruits have simmered for 5 minutes, purée them in a food processor and strain the purée. Add the sugar, reheat the purée until it simmers, and then stir in 2 tablespoons cornstarch dissolved in ⅓ cup cold water. Bring the mixture to a boil, stirring constantly, just until the cloudiness of the cornstarch disappears. Pour into serving bowls, let cool, and chill until thickened. Serve with light cream and extra sugar.

POT LUCK

MENU

◆

CHICKEN POT PIE WITH LEEKS AND WILD MUSHROOMS

◆

OVEN-BRAISED TOMATOES

◆

GREEN SALAD WITH WARM BACON DRESSING

◆

HONEY BAKED APPLES WITH CARDAMOM CUSTARD SAUCE

OPPOSITE: CHICKEN POT PIE WITH LEEKS AND WILD MUSHROOMS

$\mathcal{C}$HICKEN POT PIE WITH LEEKS AND WILD MUSHROOMS

THIS CHICKEN AND VEGETABLE STEW CAN BE ASSEMBLED, PUT IN ITS baking dish without the shortcrust dough, and refrigerated the day before it is needed but should be brought back to room temperature before cooking. The dough can be made up to 2 days ahead, wrapped in plastic wrap, and refrigerated, or made well ahead and frozen.

SHORTCRUST PASTRY DOUGH
1½ cups all-purpose flour
¼ teaspoon salt
½ cup cold lard or solid vegetable shortening, cut into 10 pieces

CHICKEN PIE FILLING
½ pound fresh edible wild mushrooms (see Note)
1 cup fresh peas, or thawed frozen peas
5 to 7 tablespoons butter
3 tablespoons vegetable oil
2 carrots, thinly sliced
2 leeks (white and pale green parts only), washed and thinly sliced
1½ pounds chicken thighs (about 12 pieces), boned and skinned
   Salt
   Freshly ground pepper
3 tablespoons flour
1½ cups chicken stock
½ cup heavy cream
¼ cup sliced green onions
3 tablespoons chopped fresh parsley
1½ tablespoons chopped fresh tarragon, or 1½ teaspoons dried
1 large egg yolk

To prepare pastry dough, combine flour and salt in a large mixing bowl. Add lard and toss to coat with flour. Work lard and flour together with your fingertips until the mixture resembles coarse crumbs. Sprinkle 3 tablespoons cold water over mixture and gather into a ball. (If dough seems too dry add an additional tablespoon cold water and blend well.) Form dough into a flat disk, wrap in plastic wrap, and refrigerate for at least 30 minutes or up to 2 days. Remove from the refrigerator 10 minutes before rolling.

Wipe mushrooms with paper towels to remove any dirt and slice.

To transform an old-fashioned chicken pot pie into a new animal altogether, substitute a trio of fish and a simple fish stock for the chicken and chicken stock.

Buy a ½-pound piece each of cod and fresh salmon and ½ pound shelled shrimp. Skin and bone the fish and cut it into 2- by 2½-inch pieces.

Sauté the shrimp in the butter and oil until they just turn pink, remove them with a slotted spoon, and set them aside.

Dip the fish in seasoned flour and sauté it in the remaining fat until the surfaces begin to brown lightly but the fish is barely cooked. Then make up the pie in the same manner as for the chicken pot pie.

If using fresh peas, place in a small saucepan of boiling water to blanch for 2 minutes; then drain and place fresh or thawed frozen peas in a 10- or 11-inch round or square baking dish (2½- to 3-quart capacity).

In a large skillet, melt 1 tablespoon of the butter with 1 tablespoon oil. Add mushrooms and sauté over medium-high heat, stirring frequently, for about 5 minutes, until they are tender and lightly browned. Remove mushrooms with a slotted spoon and place in baking dish.

Melt 4 tablespoons of the remaining butter and the remaining oil in the same skillet, add carrots and leeks, cover, and cook over low heat, stirring once or twice to prevent burning, for about 10 minutes. Remove vegetables with a slotted spoon and place in baking dish.

Cut chicken into 2-inch cubes, pat it dry with paper towels, and season lightly with salt and pepper. Place in the skillet and sauté over medium-high heat for 10 to 15 minutes, or until browned and almost cooked through. Remove with a slotted spoon and add to baking dish.

About 2 tablespoons of fat should remain in the skillet. (If not, add the remaining 2 tablespoons butter.) Stir flour into fat and cook over high heat, stirring constantly with a wooden spoon, for about 2 minutes. Gradually stir in the stock and cream and simmer, stirring and scraping up any brown bits, for about 5 minutes, or until sauce is smooth and thick.

Pour sauce into baking dish and stir gently to blend with other ingredients. Stir in green onions, parsley, and tarragon. Taste and season with additional pepper and salt, if necessary. (No more salt may be needed if canned chicken stock has been used, so season carefully.)

Preheat oven to 425 degrees F.

On a lightly floured surface, roll pastry out to a 12-inch round about ⅛ inch thick. Place over baking dish and trim pastry so that only about ½ inch extends past rim. Fold pastry under, then pinch and crimp to form a border that sits on the rim of the dish. Gather and roll out pastry scraps and cut out a small chicken or other shape to decorate the top of the pie, if desired. Cut several slashes in top of crust to allow steam to escape.

In a small bowl beat egg yolk with 2 teaspoons water and brush this glaze over top and border of pie.

Place pie in center of oven, immediately reduce heat to 375 degrees F., and bake for 40 to 50 minutes, or until the crust is a rich golden brown and the filling is bubbling. Serve hot.

— 6 SERVINGS —

Note: Use any combination of fresh, wild or domestic, mushrooms available or reconstitute 1 ounce dried wild mushrooms in hot water.

OVEN-BRAISED TOMATOES

USUALLY SERVED HOT, THESE CAN ALSO BE SERVED AT ROOM TEM-perature, particularly with cold meats.

- 5 to 6 medium ripe tomatoes (2 to 2½ pounds)
- 4 tablespoons butter
- 1 small onion, chopped (about ½ cup)
- 2 whole cloves
- 1 tablespoon firmly packed brown sugar
- ¾ teaspoon salt
- ¼ teaspoon freshly ground pepper
- ¼ cup Crabtree & Evelyn Tomato & Chilli Sauce
- 1 tablespoon minced fresh parsley

To make a more substantial dish, mix 1½ cups fine white bread crumbs with ¼ cup melted butter and 1 teaspoon dried thyme. Sprinkle this over the onions and parsley in the dish and bake the vegetables for 30 to 40 minutes, or until the crumb topping is nicely browned.

Cut tomatoes in half and gently scoop out and discard core and seeds. Cut the flesh into quarters and set aside.

Preheat oven to 375 degrees F.

In a small saucepan, melt butter over low heat. Add onion and cloves and cook over low heat for 5 minutes. Add brown sugar, salt, and pepper, stirring until sugar dissolves. Add the Tomato & Chilli Sauce.

Arrange tomato quarters in a shallow, oven-to-table baking dish. Pour onion mixture evenly over tomatoes and sprinkle with parsley. Cover baking dish with aluminum foil or lid and bake in center of oven for 20 minutes, or until tomatoes are soft but not falling apart.

Discard cloves. Serve tomatoes hot in the baking dish.

— 4 TO 6 SERVINGS —

GREEN SALAD WITH WARM BACON DRESSING

WHETHER THE SALAD IS TO BE SERVED AS ONE LARGE salad or individual ones, heat the bowl or salad plates before adding the greens.

4	cups rinsed, dried, and torn fresh spinach leaves
1	cup rinsed and dried arugula leaves, tough stems removed
1	cup rinsed, dried, and torn chicory (curly endive) leaves
6	slices bacon
1	tablespoon vegetable oil
2	tablespoons minced shallot
1	teaspoon honey
1	tablespoon coarse-grained mustard
¼	cup red-wine vinegar
	Salt
	Freshly ground pepper
1	hard-cooked large egg, finely chopped

Combine spinach, arugula, and chicory leaves in a large salad bowl and toss to mix.

In a large heavy skillet, cook bacon over medium heat until crisp, transfer to paper towels to drain, and pour all but 3 tablespoons bacon drippings from skillet. Add oil and shallot and cook over medium-low heat until shallot is softened, about 2 minutes. Reduce heat to low and whisk in honey, mustard, and vinegar. Season with salt and pepper.

Remove skillet from heat, slowly drizzle hot dressing over greens, and toss until leaves are evenly coated. Divide salad among 6 individual salad plates. Crumble a bacon slice over each serving and sprinkle each with some chopped egg.

— 6 SERVINGS —

ℋONEY-BAKED APPLES WITH CARDAMOM CUSTARD SAUCE

WARM, ROBUSTLY FLAVORED APPLES AND A DELICATE COLD SAUCE combine beautifully in this simple dessert. The sauce would be equally delicious on stewed fruits, old-fashioned pound cake, or a warm chocolate bread pudding.

CARDAMOM CUSTARD SAUCE
4   large egg yolks
3   tablespoons sugar
2   cups half-and-half
2   whole cardamom pods, cracked to expose seeds, or
    ½ teaspoon ground cardamom
½   teaspoon vanilla extract

HONEY-BAKED APPLES
6   large Golden Delicious, Rome Beauty, or other
    baking apples
¼   cup currants
¼   cup chopped pitted dried prunes
⅓   cup chopped black walnuts
2½ tablespoons finely chopped crystallized gingerroot
2   tablespoons apricot preserves
1   teaspoon freshly grated lemon zest
¼   teaspoon ground cardamom
2   tablespoons butter
⅓   cup honey
⅓   cup orange juice
1   tablespoon fresh lemon juice
¼   teaspoon ground nutmeg

In a medium mixing bowl, beat egg yolks and sugar until pale yellow and thick.

Heat half-and-half and cardamom pods in a medium-sized enamel or other non-reactive saucepan over low heat until small bubbles begin to form around edges. Remove from the heat and pour a small amount of hot mixture into egg yolk mixture, whisking constantly. Add remaining half-and-half mixture, whisking. Pour mixture back into the saucepan and cook over lowest possible heat, stirring constantly, until custard thickens and coats the back of a wooden spoon, about 10 minutes. Strain through a sieve into a bowl. Add vanilla and stir briefly to cool. Cover the surface with plastic wrap and refrigerate until cold.

Preheat oven to 350 degrees F.

Using a small knife, core apples, keeping them whole and slightly enlarging the hollow center. Remove peel from around one core end and about halfway down each apple.

In a small bowl, combine currants, prunes, walnuts, gingerroot, preserves, lemon zest, and ground cardamom and stir until well blended. Stuff mixture into cored hollows of apples, packing it down firmly and mounding a small amount on top. Place apples in a well-buttered shallow baking dish just large enough to hold them.

In a small saucepan, combine butter, honey, orange juice, lemon juice, and nutmeg and heat, stirring, over low heat until butter is melted and mixture is smooth. Pour over the apples and bake apples in the center of oven, basting every 10 minutes with pan juices, for 40 to 50 minutes, or until apples are fork tender but not mushy. Remove from the oven and let cool slightly.

To serve, pour about ¼ cup chilled cardamom custard sauce into the bottom of each of 6 dessert dishes or shallow bowls. Place an apple in the center of each dish and drizzle each with some of the pan juices.

— 6 SERVINGS —

As an alternative to the Cardamom Custard Sauce, beat 1 cup heavy cream until it holds stiff peaks. Fold in ⅓ to ½ cup Crabtree & Evelyn Fruit Only Blackcurrant Conserve. Its intense flavor provides a lovely balance to the sweet spiciness of the juices from the apples.

$\mathscr{B}$RIOCHE

AN IDEAL INTRODUCTION TO BRIOCHE MAKING, THIS RECIPE DOES not require the special fluted brioche pan. It is baked in a bread pan, and the recipe is simpler than the results suggest.

2½ to 3 cups all-purpose flour
1 ¼-ounce package quick-rising dry yeast (see Note)
1 tablespoon sugar
1 teaspoon salt
½ cup (1 stick) plus 2 tablespoons unsalted butter
4 large eggs

In a food processor fitted with the steel blade, add 2 cups of the flour, yeast, sugar, and salt and pulse to mix. In a small saucepan, heat butter and ¼ cup water until butter is melted and the mixture is hot to the touch (125 to 130 degrees F.). Pour the liquid into the dry ingredients and process for a few seconds, or until the dough begins to form into a ball. Add eggs and process for about 45 seconds, or until dough becomes smooth and sticky and begins to pull away from the side of the work bowl. If dough is too wet, add some of the remaining ½ cup flour and process for a few seconds more. Scrape dough into a buttered mixing bowl, cover with a damp cloth, and let rise in a warm place for 45 minutes to 1 hour, or until it is double in bulk.

Punch down dough and place in a buttered 8½- by 4½-inch loaf pan. Cover with a damp cloth and let rise until double in bulk again, about 30 minutes.

Preheat oven to 375 degrees F.

Place brioche in center of oven and bake for 35 to 45 minutes, or until the top is deep golden brown and the loaf sounds hollow when tapped lightly on the bottom. Turn out onto a wire rack and let cool completely before slicing.

— MAKES 1 BRIOCHE LOAF —

Note: The brioche can be made with regular active dry yeast, which requires about double the rising time of fast-rising yeast.

$\mathcal{S}$ALLY LUNN

1   cup milk
½   cup (1 stick) unsalted butter, cut into pieces
3½ to 4 cups all-purpose flour
⅓   cup sugar
1½ teaspoons salt
1   ¼-ounce package quick-rising dry yeast
3   large eggs

GLAZE
1   tablespoon sugar

In a medium saucepan, warm milk to 125 to 130 degrees F., or until hot to the touch. Add butter, remove saucepan from the heat, and set aside, stirring occasionally, until butter is melted.

In a large mixing bowl, combine 2½ cups of the flour, the sugar, salt, and yeast. Pour hot milk mixture into dry ingredients and beat for about 3 minutes, or until well blended. Add eggs and beat until smooth.

Add enough of the remaining flour, ½ cup at a time, to make a stiff batter. Cover bowl with a damp cloth and set aside to rise for 30 minutes, or until double in bulk.

Preheat oven to 375 degrees F.

Stir down batter and spoon it into two 6-inch soufflé dishes that have been generously buttered. Cover with a damp cloth and let dough rise for 20 minutes more, or until double in bulk again.

Bake in the center of oven for 35 to 40 minutes, or until the tops are a rich golden color and a skewer inserted in the centers of the bread comes out clean.

Meanwhile, prepare the glaze: Combine the sugar and 1 tablespoon water in a small saucepan and heat over medium-low heat, stirring, until sugar is dissolved. When bread is cooked, remove from the oven and brush each loaf generously with the glaze. Return loaves to the oven for 2 minutes more to dry the glaze. Turn loaves out of the pans onto a wire rack and let cool.

— MAKES 12 TO 16 SLICES —

Sally Lunn dough may also be formed into smaller buns that are split and filled with sweetened whipped cream and sugar.

$\mathscr{G}$RUYÈRE ROLLS

TO GIVE THESE ROLLS A HARD, PLEASANTLY CHEWY CRUST, USE A mister to spray the inside of the oven with water during baking.

3 cups all-purpose flour
1 ¼-ounce package quick-rising dry yeast
1 cup grated Gruyère cheese
¼ teaspoon sugar
1 teaspoon salt
1¼ cups lukewarm (105 to 115 degrees F.) water

In a large mixing bowl, combine 2¾ cups of the flour, the yeast, cheese, sugar, and salt. Add the lukewarm water and stir until well blended.

Turn dough out onto a lightly floured surface and knead for about 10 minutes, adding more flour as needed to form a smooth and elastic, medium-soft dough. Or knead the dough for 5 minutes in a heavy-duty mixer with a dough hook.

Place dough in a buttered bowl, turning to grease all sides. Cover with a damp cloth and let rise in a warm place for about 40 minutes, or until double in bulk. Punch dough down.

To shape rolls, divide dough in half, then cut each half into 8 equal pieces. Working on a lightly floured surface, roll each piece of dough into a smooth ball, then elongate slightly to form an oval. Place rolls 2 inches apart on lightly buttered baking sheets. Set them aside in a warm place and let rise for about 30 minutes, or until almost double in bulk.

Preheat oven to 425 degrees F.

Place rolls in the center of the oven and spray oven interior with water from a mister. Bake for 5 minutes and spray again. Reduce heat to 350 degrees F. and bake for 15 minutes more, or until the rolls are pale golden brown and crusty. Turn them out onto a wire rack to cool.

— MAKES 16 ROLLS —

$\mathcal{S}$ALT-CRUSTED BREAD STICKS

THESE BREAD STICKS WILL STAY FRESH FOR 2 TO 3 DAYS IN A COVERED container; they also freeze well.

1   ¼-ounce package quick-rising dry yeast
2¼ teaspoons sugar
1½ teaspoons salt
3   cups all-purpose flour
1   cup lukewarm (105 to 115 degrees F.) water
4   tablespoons olive oil
1   large egg white
1   to 2 tablespoons coarse salt

In a large mixing bowl, the bowl of an electric mixer fitted with a dough hook, or a food processor fitted with a plastic blade, combine yeast, sugar, salt, and about 2¼ cups of the flour. Add the lukewarm water and stir until well blended. Beat in olive oil, mixing until smooth. Gradually add enough of the remaining flour to make a moderately stiff dough. Knead until the dough is smooth and elastic—by hand, about 10 minutes; by machine, about 5 minutes. Place dough in an oiled bowl, turn it to coat it all over with oil, and cover with a damp cloth. Let rise in a warm place until double in bulk, about 40 minutes.

Preheat oven to 325 degrees F.

Punch dough down and divide into 24 equal pieces. Roll each piece of dough between the palms of the hands to make a "rope" about 12 inches long. (Don't worry if dough ropes are not perfectly symmetrical.) Place dough ropes 1½ inches apart on two large buttered baking sheets.

In a small bowl, whisk egg white with 1 teaspoon water until well blended. Brush a little of the egg white glaze over each dough rope and sprinkle each with some of the coarse salt.

Bake bread sticks for 30 minutes, or until golden brown, dry, and crisp. (If baking both sheets in the same oven, reverse positions halfway through baking so that the bread sticks brown evenly.) Let the bread sticks cool on wire racks.

— MAKES 24 BREAD STICKS —

WHOLE-WHEAT AND POTATO CLOVERLEAF ROLLS

Cakes and breads made with mashed potatoes have a moistness, fine texture, and keeping quality reminiscent of the best old-fashioned baking. The mashed potatoes are usually added hot or are mixed with part of the liquid; leftover mashed potatoes should never be added cold from the refrigerator.

THESE ROLLS HAVE THE AROMA OF A WHOLE-WHEAT BREAD BUT THE lightness of a traditional cloverleaf roll.

1½ cups whole-wheat flour
1½ to 1¾ cups all-purpose flour
1½ teaspoons salt
1   tablespoon sugar
1   ¼-ounce package quick-rising dry yeast
1   medium potato, boiled, peeled, and mashed with a fork
1   cup milk
4   tablespoons unsalted butter
1   large egg, lightly beaten

TO ASSEMBLE
6   tablespoons unsalted butter, melted

In a large mixing bowl, combine the whole-wheat flour with 1 cup of the all-purpose flour, the salt, sugar, and yeast.

In a small saucepan, heat the mashed potato with the milk and butter, stirring, until the butter is melted. Add potato mixture to the dry ingredients and stir until well blended. Whisk in the egg and add enough of the remaining all-purpose flour to make a soft but workable dough. Turn out onto a floured surface and knead for 8 to 10 minutes, or until smooth and elastic.

Place the dough in a buttered bowl, cover, and let rise in a warm place for 20 to 40 minutes, or until double in bulk. Punch down the dough. Lightly butter 24 muffin cups. For each roll, make three 1-inch balls of dough, rolling the dough between the palms of the hands. Dip each ball into the melted butter and tuck three into each muffin cup. Let the rolls rise in a warm place for about 10 minutes, or until almost double in bulk.

Preheat the oven to 400 degrees F.

Brush the rolls with the remaining melted butter and bake for 15 to 20 minutes, or until they sound hollow when tapped. Carefully lift each onto a wire rack to cool slightly.

— MAKES 24 ROLLS —

$\mathscr{T}$HE WELL-STOCKED PANTRY

DIAMONDS MAY BE FINE FOR SOME, BUT A dazzling pantry is the cook's best friend. Shelves brimming with herbs and spices, oils and vinegars, mustards, sauces and relishes, pastas and rices, preserved and dried fruit, sweetmeats and nuts, jams, jellies, fruit curds, and honeys compose the cook's treasury.

Even the best fresh foods, carefully prepared in their prime, benefit from gentle flavoring with something from the pantry. A drop of delicate wine or fruit vinegar, a spoonful of olive or nut oil, or hints of herbs or spices give a finishing touch. And, as the culinary calendar progresses from spring rhubarb to autumn pheasant, the addition of the pantry's bounty from other seasons and regions produces diverse and delicious results.

Happily, there is no best pantry; good ones are as individual as their owners' kitchens and cooking. And all save busy cooks time and inspired cooks time-consuming searches for ingredients. The following are some basic pantry contents and uses.

ANCHOVIES: Available as fillets packed in oil or dried salted; or as a ready-made paste in a tube.

BREAD CRUMBS: Available dried, or may be made fresh and stored in the freezer.

CAPERS: Enliven the flavor of mild, pale foods such as eggs, broiled fish, chicken fricassee, and veal paprika with these salty-sharp buds.

Sprinkle over salads or add to herbed dressings.

CHOCOLATE: Available in bitter, semisweet, unsweetened, or sweetened bars or as chocolate chips.

Fold grated bitter or semisweet chocolate into whipped cream to serve with custard, rice pudding, tapioca, or fruit.

CHUTNEYS: Available fruited (English style) and with only mango (Indian style).

Use as a seasoning for sauces to be served with roasted or broiled meat.

Season mayonnaise with a few spoonfuls.

Mix into raw ground beef for hamburgers, allowing about 2 teaspoons for each burger.

COCOA: Available in various qualities; always buy the best, unsweetened.

COOKIES: Keep special homemade ones in the freezer; on the pantry shelf store best-quality commercial butter cookies or macaroons in sealed containers.

Extend the number of servings for a mousse or pudding by layering it with macaroons, lightly sprinkling the cookies with flower water or a liqueur if desired.

CORN: Buy canned kernels or jars of baby ears of corn.

CORN SYRUP: Available light and dark.

Substitute corn syrup for sugar in baked fruit desserts and pies for a subtly different sweetness.

CRANBERRIES: Keep raw whole cranberries in the freezer; good-quality canned cranberry sauce on the shelf.

For a different, easy fruit crumble, mix equal amounts of halved pitted plums and whole cranberries, following the instructions on page 89 for Rhubarb Crumble.

Stir into applesauce for heightened flavor.

CREAM: Available heavy (whipping) and light.

FLOUR: Always keep all-purpose unbleached white, cake, and whole-wheat at least; consider buckwheat, rye, and graham flours for more diverse baking.

FRUIT: Keep fresh (whole or puréed) in the refrigerator; best-quality commercial or home-preserved, along with dried fruit such as apricots, apples, pears, prunes, raisins, and currants, on the shelf.

Enhance bottled fruit by preserving in a liqueur. Serve with unsweetened whipped cream and cinnamon toast fingers. Or savor a small glass of fruit and liqueur after dinner.

FRUIT SYRUPS: On a hot day, stir 2 to 3 tablespoons fruit syrup into a glass of still or sparkling water for a delicate, refreshing drink.

GARLIC: Mash 2 to 4 peeled garlic cloves with ½ teaspoon salt and add to a mayonnaise. Eat with cold meat, steamed vegetables, salads, or smoked fish.

GELATIN

GINGERROOT: Keep the fresh root in the refrigerator; store gingerroot that is preserved in syrup or crystallized on the shelf.

Slice preserved ginger and sprinkle over peeled, sliced oranges.

HERBS: Keep dried herbs, such as bay leaf, *bouquet garni*, celery seed, mint, oregano, rosemary, sage, tarragon, and thyme on the shelf; keep fresh herbs, including parsley, and herb butters in the refrigerator.

HONEY

HORSERADISH: Available bottled; buy as strong and clear-flavored as possible.

JAMS, JELLIES, AND PRESERVES: Fill a chocolate layer cake with orange marmalade.

Thin preserves slightly with brandy, kirsch, whiskey, Amaretto, or rum to make a filling for crêpes.

Instead of the usual apricot glaze, finish French apple tarts with a blackberry glaze.

MOLASSES

MUSHROOMS: Available dried (many varieties) for shelf storage.

MUSTARDS: Dry English; prepared English and French, including plain and flavored Dijon-style and coarse-grained.

Mix equal quantities of honey and prepared mustard to make a glaze for roast ham.

Season a béchamel sauce for cooked onions, endive, or cauliflower with 2 to 3 teaspoons of Dijon-style or full-flavored coarse-grained mustard to give piquancy to the dish.

OATMEAL: Store old-fashioned rolled oats.

OILS: Keep light vegetable oil, olive oil, walnut oil, hazelnut oil, and oil seasoned with herbs and spices on the shelf (especially advisable for walnut and hazelnut oils).

Sautéed foods are less likely to burn if equal amounts of oil and butter are used.

Use hazelnut or walnut oils in salads of tender greens, walnuts, and feta or goat cheese.

OLIVES: Keep plain green and black, Niçoise, and green stuffed with pimiento, almonds, or anchovies.

PASTA: Keep the dried in the pantry, the fresh in the freezer.

PEPPERCORNS: Keep black, white, green, red, and mixed (with spices).

PICKLES: Store homemade or best-quality commercial bread-and-butter, dill, watermelon, and cornichons; also pickled peaches, pears, and apples.

PINE NUTS: Add to stuffings for chicken, lamb, and vegetables.

Gently brown in butter and sprinkle over green vegetables just before serving or over a spinach, bacon, and hard-boiled egg salad.

PULSES: Available dried and canned, including lentils, green and white haricots, chick-peas, kidney, navy, and pinto beans.

QUAIL'S EGGS: Available bottled.

Spread a bite-size round or square of black bread with a lemony mayonnaise and top it with a slice of smoked trout and half a quail's egg.

RAISINS: Keep seeded ones for old-fashioned fruitcakes and plum puddings; seedless for other cooking and snacks.

Soak seedless raisins in brandy or rum for an hour and fold them into good-quality coffee or chocolate ice cream.

RICE: Stock long and short-grained white, natural brown, Italian arborio for risottos, and basmati for Indian dishes.

SALT: Sea salt is best.

SAUCES: Keep a selection of homemade or commercial ones, such as Cumberland, tartar, Worcestershire, and tomato (including plain ketchup and chili ketchup).

SPICES: Keep a variety, such as allspice, caraway, cardamom, cayenne, cinnamon (sticks and ground), cloves, coriander, cumin, curry powder, ground ginger, juniper, nutmeg (whole and ground), paprika, peppercorns, and hot red pepper flakes.

Crush a few allspice berries into a beef stew.

Grate nutmeg over hot Brussels sprouts.

SUGAR: Keep granulated white, light brown, dark brown, and powdered.

TOMATOES: Keep canned Italian plum tomatoes, tomato purée, and tomato juice, plus sun-dried tomatoes.

VINEGAR: Store red- and white-wine vinegars, plain and flavored, plus Sherry, balsamic, fruit, malt, and cider vinegars.

Sprinkle tarragon vinegar over hot or cold steamed green beans as a change from butter or a vinaigrette.

After sautéeing fish or meat, deglaze the skillet with a fruit or herbed wine vinegar to give zest to the pan juices.

Stir a few drops strawberry, raspberry, or black-currant vinegar into compotes of very ripe, sweet fruit such as strawberries, raspberries, pineapples, peaches, and nectarines.

WALNUTS: Sauté the nuts lightly in butter until they are golden and fragrant; then sprinkle them over hot carrots, zucchini, or any vegetables in a béchamel sauce.

YEAST: Keep quick-rising and regular active dry.